NIKOS KAZANTZAKIS

JOURNEY TO

TRANSLATED FROM THE GREEK BY F. A. REED

PHOTOGRAPHS BY ALEXANDER ARTEMAKIS

SIMON AND SCHUSTER / NEW YORK / 1965

THE

MOREA

SECOND PRINTING

LIBRARY OF CONGRESS CATALOG CARD NUMBER: 65-11981
MANUFACTURED IN THE UNITED STATES OF AMERICA
BY H. WOLFF BOOK MFG. CO., N. Y.
DESIGNED BY EDITH FOWLER

■ CONTENTS

■ SETTING OUT

■ THE FACE of Greece is a palimpsest bearing twelve successive inscriptions: Contemporary; the period of 1821; the Turkish yoke; the Frankish sway; the Byzantine; the Roman; the Hellenistic epoch; the Classic; the Dorian middle ages; the Mycenaean; the Aegean; and the Stone Age.

Pause on a patch of Greek earth and anguish overcomes you. It is a deep, twelve-leveled tomb, from which voices rise up calling to you. Which voice should you choose? Every voice, every spirit longs for its body; your heart is shaken, and cannot decide. For a Greek, the journey through Greece is a fascinating, exhausting ordeal. The voices that fascinate most are not those which awaken the loftiest and most uncompromising ideals in his mind; and yet he is ashamed to make the gesture of wakening those less important, though still beloved departed. As you stand beside a flowering rhododendron of the Eurotas River, between Sparta and Mistra, the frightful, ageless struggle between heart and mind is joined. Your full heart leaps forward to resurrect a pale, death-destined body; it wants to turn back the wheel of time to the sixth of January, 1449, when

7

here, high up at Mistra, that body accepted the tormented, short-lived crown. A host of paternal groans, murmurs of demotic songs, and longings of the Race impel you to make the gesture; but the mind resists, and turning toward Sparta it becomes fierce, struggles to surmount this sentimental nostalgia and to mingle with the eternal youths.

For a foreigner the pilgrimage to Greece is simple, it happens without any great convulsion; his mind, liberated from sentimental entanglements, leaps on to discover the essence of Greece. But for the Greek, this pilgrimage is fraught with hopes and fears, with distress and painful comparison. Never does a clear and unencumbered thought arise, never a bloodless impression. A Greek landscape does not give us—if we know how to listen and to love—an innocent tremor of beauty. The landscape has a name, it is bound up with a memory— here we were shamed, here glorified; blood or sacred statues rise up from the soil, and all at once the landscape is transformed into rich, all-encompassing History, and the Greek pilgrim's whole spirit is thrown into confusion.

Merciless questions arise to lash our brains. How were so many wonders created, and what are we ourselves doing? Why has the race become debased? How can we carry on once more? You ask, ask again, you bend down to gaze at the living countenances you encounter on the street, prick up your ears to hear what they say, hold your breath expecting to grasp a movement, a thought, a cry that will give you courage.

The journey through Greece is transformed into the laborious, persevering quest of hope. Walk through Corinth, Argos, Olympia, Megalopolis and Sparta, and an unexpected responsibility weighs on your shoulders; on the shoulders of all the living Greeks around you. The names have a strange and irresistible power—whoever is born in Greece, whether or not he so wishes, undertakes great responsibility.

My own journey in the Peloponnesos, stormy with such concerns, gave me many delights, and sorrows. From the first moments, as I was heading for the station, a fond shade leaped up to accompany me. As often as I tour through Greece, this lithe and slender shadow nearly always stretches out beside mine on the soil and rocks: Ion Dragoumis.[1] No one else could appreciate more taciturnly, with more detachment and more restrained passion, the instant that we leave Attica and begin the journey. Because Attica had the profoundest correspondence with his being, so dry, filled with naked, shining stones and hidden, fascinating greenery. Some of his words come to mind at the moment of departure, giving me delight and great excitement: "Like a warm and mighty river Hellenism with its archons flows." You sense this phrase like a great vein within you, branching and coursing; and in some mysterious way it helps you to see and to comprehend Greece.

Crowded in among clamoring, sweating, newspaper- and basket-laden householders, I watch Attica slipping away behind me, dematerialized in the light. In every Greek landscape, but even more so here in Attica, the light is the protagonist-hero. The mountains, the valley and the sea form the arena in which he struggles, or the couch on which he reposes. The mountains, the valley, the sea play a secondary role. The light is the resplendent Sober Dionysos who is dismembered and suffers, then rejoins his parts and triumphs. The entire scene of Greece seems to have come to be just so that he might perform. Noon nears, shadows curl up around the tree roots. Eleusis, excavated and gaping open, glistens, mysterious no longer; the pine needles drip light; wounded and vintaged vineyards have turned brown; must reeks; bearded, rough-hewn villagers are seated in the shade, in the dionysian air, chattering in Albanian, good-natured and beastlike, with a powerful winebarrel stench, like satyrs.

Around me in the railway carriage the first conversations are begun, newspapers are folded, discussion gets under way. A skinny, dark old man in a high starched collar, with tiny eyes, turns to his neighbor, a pudgy little fellow, bald and unshaven. It seems that they are carrying on some conversation. I listen as he tells the other sententiously:

"Max Nordau said, 'Four things will destroy the world—syphilis, alcohol, malarial fever and life in the big cities.' "

Max Nordau! How many years has it been since I'd heard of that antediluvian mammoth of sociology! Today other gods reign, no one any longer dares invoke the *Conditional Lies of Society* of the Viennese Jew. He'd be ashamed. But the dead gods invariably find final refuge in the provinces. Where else is Darwin's theory alive today, the philosophy of Taine or Spencer, the poetry of Achilles Paraschos? In the quiet, languid, enchanting provinces—where learned young men or aged doctor-philosophers sit in the pastry shops or the pharmacies and debate the great issues. I realized as I listened to my neighbors that I had already crossed the borders, that I had entered the provinces at last.

High noon. The light falls vertically, this is the most Greek of hours. The perfectly classic. A little later the dusk will bring romantic shadows, will envelop the pure, severe nudity of the Greek earth in chiaroscuro effects, and break the steady, certain lines. This meridian sun is the true ancient Greek. Dusk, the night and the moon all belong to the sorceresses of Thessaly and Thrace, and to far-northern romantics.

I gaze about me. Frightening, sun-drenched emptiness. It was as if Greece had suddenly been destroyed, as if the overwhelming light had devoured her at last. Only an occasional goat munches here and there on earth's last sprig of green. A shepherd boy cocks his arm to heave a stone at us, but holds back; his instinct changes direction and content, becomes more modern, he shouts:

"A cigarette! Just a little butt, lads!"

"Bravo!" another traveler says to me. "They don't throw stones any more. Little by little we're becoming civilized. . . ."

But I didn't answer him. What could I say? That I would prefer an attack to the begging; barbaric outburst to modern degradation? If civilization means discipline of primordial instinct, then civilization has value only when the disciplined instinct serves some purpose broader and more demanding than the individual. Otherwise it is regression, sloth and cowardice.

We crossed the Isthmus and entered the Acropolis of Greece. The Peloponnesos has always been regarded as the cradle of Hellenism; sacred, fruitful earth, with all the delights of both island and mainland. The "long-suffering Morea" has been dealt all the blows of calamity and glory, from the aged grandfather of Agamemnon, to the Old Man of the Morea. A journey in Greece must always begin from the Peloponnesos, the old mother. Here are the famished, bloodstained roots —the Taygetos mountains, the Alpheos and Eurotas rivers, the Atreids, Helen, Plethon, Palaiologos, Kolokotronis. Athens, the bloom, the root's uppermost aspiration, comes later.

White, sun-baked soil, dust-filled air; a pine tree refreshes and consoles the eye like a jug of water. Corinth, newly rebuilt after the earthquakes, appears deserted, symmetrical in the dust. It spreads out silent in the sun, and only in the station at its edge do wild voices burst out; foxy Moreotes hawk grapes, the passengers descend upon a filthy long table with water and *loukoumi*. In a corner in the sunlight, a horrible cloud of smoke puffs up; a greasy kilt-clad man skewers little lumps of meat on thin reeds and pats them with sage and pepper. In the shade beneath the canopy a buxom

woman with gold teeth shakes and wriggles, staring at
the men. A soldier boy buys two *souvlakia*, two pieces
of bread and two bunches of grapes and approaches her,
coughing slyly.

Beyond, off toward the south, savage in the light,
with a metallic-blue glare, rises the Acrocorinthos, with
the weighty Byzantine, Frankish and Turkish crown
high atop its head. And at its feet, lower on the cape,
gleams the devastated region where the ancient city of
sensual joy, full of merchants, libertines and painted
women, once buzzed. The temple of Aphrodite with
the thousand priestesses, where the multibreasted Syr-
ian Astarte sought shelter, has disappeared. The decor-
ous temple of Athena Chalintida (the Bridle Holder),
who helped Bellerophon subdue Pegasus by bridling
him, has also vanished. Only the Draconera remains,
the sacred font of Peirene that Pegasus caused to flow
as he kicked the arid rock in fury.

Another time, I recall, I had gone up to the ancient
city, and had descended into the hewn rock itself to
glimpse the pure, divine spring of Poetry. For thousands
of years Bellerophon has fascinated those who strive
after the impossible with his cruel and inexorable fate.
He had leaped astride Poetry's fearful steed, but he forgot the gift of the goddess of caution, the bridle. And
thus without bridle he soared aloft, secured only by the
wings of his horse, to ravage the sky. Zeus, the ruthless
god of discipline, hurled him from Pegasus down to
earth. And Bellerophon thus wandered for the rest of
his life, blinded and crippled on the thirsting plain.

And now, in the colorful bustle of the railway station,

the greasy smoke rising from the *souvlakia,* amid the laughter that has begun to gush from the gold-toothed mouth of the plump woman munching beside the sly soldier, the cruel fate of the ancient forebear returns to mind and labors to bridle the heedless longings of the heart. But in vain. A proud, scornful voice, like the hiss of the snake of Paradise, starts up in man's bowels and whispers him the great and dangerous counsel: Do not listen to the god of discipline, be not afraid. Open your eyes, look! Better to glimpse the terrible secret and be blinded than keep your eyes unscathed, protected, limited to the lawful circle of human possibility.

Likewise the prodigal son, who returns shattered by his arrogant adventure, counsels his younger brother not to leave the paternal home. But the younger brother looks far away beyond the open door, toward the endless road. Misfortunes must never become lessons, the great irrational adventure must be eternally renewed; this is the only way, bloody but worthy of man, for him to combat his fate. Only in this way can human limitations one day be transposed and broadened.

Sophocles and Euripides, who wrote tragedies with Bellerophon as hero, would certainly censure and chastise him for his *hybris,* because he dared to desire the impossible. He violated the order of the world, forgot the prudent human commandment: *Nothing in excess.* But a contemporary soul would extol this blinded ravisher and transgressor, because our own age smolders with the same bellerophondian craving: *Everything in excess!*[2]

At that very moment the plump woman broke into a nervous laugh. Bellerophon dissipated in air, Pegasus swirled like water and vanished. I turned; the woman had jumped up and lifted her bare arm, abruptly she removed the comb that held her hair in place, moved her head up and down and shook it, and the hair leaped down over her shoulders, cascading like deep blue water. She gripped the comb in her teeth and with her two hands gathered up her hair again, arranged it and planted the comb atop it. Then she sat down beside the soldier once more.

Never will I forget that movement, so primitive and provocative. The soldier turned pale, Corinth suddenly took on meaning again. The train whistled, we clambered aboard; the soldier and the woman remained, silent and sullen, like two beasts ready to bite each other.

■ THE GULF OF CORINTH

■ THE CHARM of the Gulf of Corinth is serene and inexhaustible. A profound Mediterranean joy for the eye. On the left the pine, the olive tree, the vineyard. Dry, yellow-white earth, rocks burnished by the sun. On the right the sparkling sea, eternally renewed, carefree, smiling without memory. How could she sustain and remember the furrows traced by ancient prows across her breasts! She would be filled with wrinkles; but she forgets and preserves her youth.

In the distance the ethereal blue mountains shimmer, as if evaporating in the light. Stark naked, sunning themselves like athletes! No matter how many times you view this spectacle, your heart cannot be sated. The Greek landscape affects man's soul—his soul, his body and his most hidden thoughts—like music. You sense it more profoundly each time, better harmonize yourself with it, and discover new modes of balance and freedom.

I watched the distant, serene mountains, the smiling sea, the sparsely leafed, brightly lit trees. What nobility and simplicity, what lack of rhetoric and bombast! Everything is cut to man's measure; you reach the ideal over untroubled paths, far from the precipices. Beauty strolls over the rosy stones as does Victory, without wings, comfortably accommodated in the calm, human landscape.

Never have strength and gracefulness intermingled so organically as here, in austere and cheerful Greece. In order to comprehend ancient Greece, her thought, her art, her gods, there is only one point of departure: the soil, stone, water and air of Greece. Here you must begin. The sternest emotion, the most daring fantasy, in order to live—or better still, in order to be born—requires a body. The creator discovers its body only by looking about him, how the light plays, how the mountains stand immobile. Around him the artist searches for all his material. If his locale is of marble, or granite, or only mud, his art assumes the correspondingly different approach. The quality and resistance of matter determine not only his methods, but his heart as well. There is no closed, impassable barrier between artist and landscape. The landscape penetrates the artist's body through its five portals and fashions his senses; and, as it fashions them, a likeness is formed in their image.

My heart is disturbed as I consider our contemporary spiritual life—our thought and art. Would that the landscape were omnipotent—what bliss! This soil would unceasingly bring forth great masters. But creation is the result of complex laws, an exceptional balance between scores of visible and concealed opposing forces, an instant with no return! Only once in Greece

—thousands of years ago—did this sacred moment flash. And it endured no longer than fifty years. The landscape, before and after, remains the same, but the soul that confronts it becomes confused.

Around me in the train meaningless chatter, weary commonplaces. No one mouths a single word of substance, no one reads a book, no one gazes at the land or toward the sea with an unsullied cheerful eye. Not a single correspondence between man and landscape.

I enjoyed a few old men sitting around a *katostariko*[1] of retsina sipping, watching the passersby and shaking with laughter. In many Peloponnesian villages these old men were my sole companions. When illness had not shattered them they laughed, told tales, and looked back over life as though it were a game. Perhaps because at last they had escaped from daily cares; their sons, or their sons-in-law, had snatched their property and now gave them a lump of bread to eat and a mattress on which to sleep. And thus, carefree at last, relieved of daily troubles, they could gaze serenely at the world and laugh.

Whoever has a field, says Buddha, thinks of the field, dreams of the field, becomes the field. Only he who has nothing can be free.

Dusk. In the harbor at Aighio big barges gleamed, black and purple on an indigo sea. Cypresses stood vertical, unbending, and like black columns etched the orange of evening. The air smelled of must and vineyard.

It was night when we reached Patra. Lights, chairs,

coffeeshops, phonographs, the lingering odor of tar and jasmine at the harbor; evening strollers on the mole, ships, barges, little barks with white sails, and in them dandyish fops returning from their seagoing jaunts. In front of me an elderly matron, between her two daughters, was heading for the *kafeneion* on the mole. Here and there I snatched up a shred of conversation: "Once in a while the potatoes won't boil . . ." "This puzzle of a comb!" "But, poor mother, can't you see that . . ." "As long as you're not closefisted with your money, you'll find . . ."

I roamed about next day from the morning on, avidly going up and down the streets, as if for the first time beholding the spectacle of the province.

I climb the stairs and reach the fortress. Wild and deserted, with toppled towers, fearsome encircling battlements, besieged and now overrun by fragrant greens —caper, mint, sage. In other times Romans, Saracens, Franks, Slavs and Turks stormed this fortress. Now all these ephemeral besiegers have vanished and the lawful inhabitants have remained—the caper, mint and sage. Fragments of ancient columns have been erected on the north wall. Here on this acropolis the temple of Lu phraea Artemis, to whom fruits and catches of the hunt were proffered, once stood.

The city spreads out below, full of greenery, with broad straight streets right up to the sparkling sea. The day is mild and autumnal, the sky lightly clouded—a few drops had fallen in the morning. The tree leaves are beginning to turn red, a few grapes still hang in long bunches from trellised vines. On just such a fall day, pervaded with tenderness, the great lovers—Antony and Cleopatra—arrived, to spend the entire winter in Patra. They meandered through these streets, she in a gilded litter borne by gigantic Negroes, and he beside her astride his horse. And it seemed to me that I heard their Shakespearean words, hers supplicating and affectionate, his mild and muted:

> *Then was the time for words; no going then:*
> *Eternity was in our lips and eyes,*
> *Bliss in our brows bent . . .*

And he raised high his hand in the wind and pledged to her:

> *. . . by the fire*
> *That quickens Nilus' slime, I go from hence.*
> *Thy soldier, servant, making peace or war*
> *As thou affect'st.*

Noon: I went down to the mole where the Patrians were hurrying to sip *ouzo*, munch *loukoumi* and listen to music. I sat down next to three little old ladies. My back was turned and I watched an English ship making ready to leave. I read the tall gold letters on the stern: FLAMINIA, LIVERPOOL, and set free my mind to break quietly away from Patra and soar off. The air smelled of sea and sweat. The proprietor of the *kafeneion* had spread out his mattress and sheets in the sun. Another elderly lady came up and took a seat beside my three neighbors. She unfolded a newspaper.

"What's new, Mrs. Victoria?" they ask her.

"Well, nothing much, Mrs. Virginia," she replies with a sigh. "Nothing of importance. War in China, thousands being killed, they say Russia will help and another World War will be touched off. In Spain the same thing all over again. Nothing of importance."

One of the little old ladies protested:

"What are you saying, Mrs. Victoria? Nothing of importance? But didn't you read yesterday's police order then, that all dogs must be destroyed? My poor Lulu . . ."

A young man with greasy, heavily oiled hair, bright eyes, broad cuffs and baggy trousers, erotic and pernicious, appeared on the scene. Through curled, aristocratic lips he sang a frivolous, impudent popular song; musicians behind him, with white kerchiefs around their throats for the sweat, accompanied on violins and bass viols. The sea simmered and reeked of rotten watermelon, tomatoes bobbed on the swell, mustachioed men cracked sunflower seeds and spat far in the direction of the water.

The song came to a halt; a pale, thin young woman clad in black leaped onto the stage. Behind her two macabre young men appeared, with somber expressions and long frock coats, like undertakers. I started. But the woman began to dance, the two youths jumped forward and grabbed her, and the pale prize fell first into the grasp of one, then darted shrieking into the embrace of the other.

By evening all the ennui of provincial life had finally settled into me. Dullness, a peculiar sweetness, and wearied summation. In Patra, and at Pyrgos, Tripolis, Sparta, Argos and Nafplio on other days, I lived the fervid dullness of the sluggish provincial climate, where the young re-enumerate with burning fingers their never-changing moments. Here a youth can rapidly become an automaton, completely entangled in clockwork habits. But simultaneously, through reaction, pride and stubbornness, he can amass silent, unused longing and strength; his heart can expand and then explode in a masterful verse, in a courageous act, in a creation filled with virtuous isolation. Spiritual and ethical *decency*, the priceless bashfulness of youth, the sacred "down" of spiritual purity, finds shelter only in the provinces. In a great city the child is born without this down, his eyes and ears are soon corrupted, and this precocious maturity deforms his soul.

In the provinces, amid silent lanes, in spotless flowerpot-filled courtyards, on peaceful country strolls, in the craving of expectation and the difficulty of satisfying every aspiration, the youth finds time to desire. A great distance exists between desire and the realization of that desire, and in traversing this distance, a youth belabors and stimulates his highest abilities. For a short while natural youthful elation for the higher things manages to endure, and in living for that short time it matures, is strengthened, and is less easily compromised.

So, as the capitals have lost their innocence, the only

remaining hope for the renewal of Earth's virginity has taken refuge in the modest, languid and enchanting province.

■ THE FORTRESSES
OF THE MOREA

■ FORTRESSES EXERT a mysterious fascination on man's soul. When a precipitous mountain suddenly rises up from the valley at the horizon's depth, and when you distinguish a crown of half-toppled walls, towers, and bastions at its peak, your soul leaps up emboldened. In your imagination it girds on its arms and is prepared to make—and then to carry out—great decisions. The low-lying, chastened plain with its swamps and foothills, and the peak with its bold crown, are the visible representation of the human soul. Paths are laid down within us, villages built, men and beasts file past, we give up everything; but we should like to preserve the highest, most inaccessible stronghold of our soul untouched. The fortress reminds us of that fortified point that we want never to surrender, the last refuge of conscience, self-respect and courage.

When suddenly we glimpse a deserted fortress from afar, isolated, abandoned in the lofty air of the summit, an inarticulate voice, a warlike shout soars, beyond our will, from our breast. Just as poetry is no more than the analysis of a moan or joyous cry by musical lan-

guage, so also is this inarticulate voice; if we could ana-
lyze it, it would create a whole, strict system of ethics.
The soul would appear to us as an uphill assault, and
life as a mobilization of men.

Rarely, though, do city dwellers behold fortresses,
and the thought that they are surrendering all the
strongholds within them to the enemy rarely comes to
denounce them as deserters.

Clermont, Karytaina, Nikli, Geraki, Mistra, Methoni,
Koroni, Monemvasia—they still stand, erect like sen-
tinels searching the air, which is now vacant of grandeur. I'd left Patra and entered the rich Achaian plain,
with its vineyards, olives, quince trees and cypresses.
Wonderful figs and grapes, the landscape calm, deep
green.

Lekhaina. A sizable church, houses among the trees;
like a flash of lightning the shade of Andreas Karkavitsas[1] beckoned in the air. Pointed beard, savages, innocent eye, and bitter smile. It flickered for an instant
in the light and vanished.

I reached Andravida, the renowned medieval capital
of the Franks. Its Frankish churches have disappeared,
swallowed by the earth; the tombs of the first three Villehardouins, the princes of the Morea, have vanished as
well. Now the men are playing cards in the *kafeneions*,
and the coarse, sun-wrinkled women are hunched over
raisins spread out in the fields; from time to time they
cry out in piercing voices. Humorless and harsh, they
work ceaselessly, and stare without smiling at a visitor.

Here a smile is one of the rarest phenomena. Sometimes they laugh boisterously, but their faces are nearly always sullen and gloomy. Not once in my entire journey in the Peloponnesos did I encounter a calm, benevolent, well-meaning and earnest smile. Neither the smile of the primitive, artless *kouros*, which flows from the balanced ease of still virgin strength; with this smile great civilizations begin. Nor the smile of a perfectly cultured man, who, having sampled and enjoyed everything, returns cured from all chimeras and confronts the world smiling; thus all great civilizations end. Contemporary Greeks have no such smiles. They are neither guileless nor thoroughly civilized. They are still in midjourney, in the midst of the battle, the dark struggle. Not for a single instant can they forget themselves. No longer artless, but still not cultured, they cannot smile.

Hurriedly I left Andravida. The flatlands were stifling me. I longed to reach the famous fortress of Clermont[2] near Glarenza. An exquisite valley, delicate nature, fertile earth. From the train a stretch of scorched earth appears. Flames soar up, tree branches crackle, smoke covers the sun. The train passed for an instant through the flames. Joyously the heart leaps up; flames always bring it an inexplicable, barbarous delight. Man's heart is much older than his mind, it remembers and longs for the joys which it once felt, thousands of years ago, in primeval caves, on the lakes, in the forests. Mind labors to bring it up to date, to give it a modern character, to stifle its shouts. But as soon as the heart catches sight of flames consuming trees or houses, as soon as it sees blood flowing or touches a woman in the dark, it begins to cry out.

At the village of Kavasilas we stopped to await the tiny local train that would take us to Kyllini, the Glarenza of old. By then it was dusk, we sat down in a wretched *kafeneion* near the coaches. Cool water, grapes, figs—nothing of the kind. Only coffee and *loukoumi*. I lighted my pipe, my faithful traveling companion, and a strange emotion seized me. Perhaps because I was alone in an unknown village and night was falling. Two villagers came over to me and opened a conversation. One was pale, hunchbacked, with tiny, melancholy eyes; the other one plump and paunchy. Where am I from, what sort of work do I do, why am I wandering about, what's my name, all the venerable questions. They learned everything, the crust was broken, real conversation could begin. The fat man placed his sweating hand on my knee and began to relate an endless, nauseating adventure. He had eczema all over his body, it was driving him mad. He visited the doctor at Lekhaina—nothing. He went as far as Patra —nothing. Finally he visited the *kafetzoudes*.[3]

"To the *kafetzoudes!*" I exclaimed.

"Don't laugh!" said the fat one, wrinkling his brows. "They've got a *tanagra* in them."

Delighted, I perked up. This is how words are created.

"A *tanagra!*" I said. "What's that?"

"Why, it's another soul that sees!"

Let Mr. Tanagra's bones dance! His name has

reached fame's loftiest peak: it has become a common noun. A tiny doll-like spirit, like a tanagraic *Kore*, residing in the warm and mysterious breasts of the *kafet-zoudes*, and seeing everything.

The fat man opened his jacket, rolled up his trousers and showed me his bare and flabby flesh, so that I'd believe him.

"You see? Not a thing! Spotless!"

We fell silent. I ordered more *loukoumi* and water; dusk had already fallen, it became cooler, the hour for confessions. The melancholy hunchback drew his chair closer.

"You seem to be a good man. I've some advice to ask of you," he said, lowering his voice. "Charitos knows."

Charitos was the fat one with eczema. He nodded his head and sighed.

"Speak up, Demo," he said. "Talk, poor devil, talk—relieve yourself."

"I've got a woman like cool water. My father was well off, she was poor, she married me. What I haven't done to please her! Whatever she could want. Dresses, patent-leather shoes, white bread—I've even gotten her a maid. Her hand never touches cold water. What can she be missing? Nothing! She's got everything, everything. Why, she butters her bread on both sides. What's missing?"

The fat fellow coughed and glanced at me knowingly. But I had already sunk deep into the calamity of the hunchback and didn't have the heart to laugh. I knew what she was missing, but said nothing. The hunchback continued:

"I'm in business as a broker, making the rounds of the villages; I get as far as Pyrgos. When I get home my wife leans out the window and yells: 'Back again? Get out! I don't want you!' And the neighbors hear her, of course. So I double over and sneak into my own house, trembling. 'If you love someone else,' I tell her, 'tell me. It doesn't matter. Love him. But don't leave me!'"

The hunchback's voice was quavering. Charitos slapped his plump thighs and burst out laughing.

"Well, poor Demo, it serves you right. Is that the way to handle women? I had one with her nose in the air, with an aristocratic upbringing. A lean, touchy noblewoman. One day she says to me: 'But at my father's house . . .' And, by God, she said nothing else. But I was looking for an excuse, I wanted to find the opportunity to lay her out with a beating. So that she'd know how things are. 'Aha!' I shouted. 'So, eh? At your father's house, eh?' And I grabbed a stick of wood. 'I give you this one, that one's a gift!' And did she say another word? Not a peep! I strung a cord through that stick and hung it above the door. So she'd see it, and remember. That's what women need, poor Demo. Punishment, I tell you!"

The hunchback shook his head, rolled his eyes and looked at me. I shall never forget the sorrow, the desperate plea, the anguish of his gaze. In the deepening night, in this wretched *kafeneion* by the railway coaches, in the unknown village of Kavasilas, a man begged your help. He will have told all his fellow villagers of his suffering, and they will have mocked him; and now the unfortunate soul flings himself upon the first stranger to offer him a lump of *loukoumi*, and tells him of his misery, to ease the pain.

"What'll I do?" he said after some time. "What advice could you give me?"

What could he do! I kept silent and looked off at a poplar tree across the way, and to a fragrant blossoming oleander. The odor was like bitter almond. I recalled sandy shores with oleanders and frolicking children, and two horses that I once saw, swimming and neighing. Their shining heads rose above the waves, their necks twisted right and left and their lower lips quivered with sensual joy.

"Leave her!" fat Charitos cried out.

"I can't," the hunchback murmured.

And he turned once more toward me.

"What am I to do?" he asked me again with anguish.

"The train!" shouted a railroad employee as he beat the gong.

I got up. The hunchback did not move. Silent, motionless, he watched me leave. As though he were watching his last hope disappear.

Charitos scurried to take my bags, helped me into the carriage and winked at me.

"Serves him right!" he said. "He shouldn't have married her. After all, he's a hunchback. What does he want with a woman? But since he's got her, he ought to beat her. He's a man, isn't he? Beating! And what do you have to say?"

Everything is right in this variegated, irrational, incredibly rich world. Just as a basinful of water becomes salty when a grain of salt is dissolved in it, so truth is dispersed everywhere, imperceptible, penetrating, saline like a tear.

When the train began to pull away, I was relieved. I had evaded both questions, had avoided stretching out my hand to interfere and thus narrow the realm of truth and falsehood. The hunchback will continue to refine his miserable life, passing it through misfortune's fine-meshed filter; and fat Charitos, tranquil at last beside his subdued and happy wife, will gaze at the "blessed" wood that hangs from a cord above the door. And both of them serve out well their obligations upon this fickle and fascinating earth.

Night had fallen, I could discern nothing. Now and again a station, activity, noise, lanterns, shining eyes, hands reaching from the train. The darkness came alive for an instant, then all at once lanterns and voices vanished again, and we rolled on, silent, toward the sea.

Kavasilas! With sudden illumination the word came to my mind again. Now I understand why an inexplicable emotion had gripped me as I sat in the sorry *kafeneion*. But the two villagers, with their human afflictions, had come and led my thoughts astray. Now, as I remained alone, liberated, my mind lit up. The name of the village had brought unconsciously to my memory an old and revered figure, a great, long-forgotten Byzantine mystic, Nikolaos Kavasilas. He was the author of a remarkable book. One evening, sitting in the cell of a Holy Mountain monastery, I read it.

Pater Arsenios, a thin and yellow monk, held a candle

nearby, casting a light. I read in a loud voice, and Arsenios, though he heard, could understand nothing; and because he understood nothing, his ardor leaped forward unhindered and soared full-winged into its paradise. He wept at my side as he heard the incomprehensible phrases, and the candle shook. I grasped his arm to steady it; even now I recall some of the lofty precepts, filled with pride and abnegation, which the Godobsessed mystic had whispered to Arsenios and to me:

"This world labors unceasingly with the birthpangs of the new man . . . Not only did he bring new light, but he created a new eye . . . The body is humble stuff, it vibrates, and does not leave the divine seal intact." And at last I remembered that exceptional phrase which has so benefitted my life. Extremely difficult, but he alone who is able to live it, to live it every moment, can become a free man: *"I believe that I am wreathed, while others are victorious."*

Thus, alone in the coach, deep in the night, I skimmed the pages of my memory as the hours passed. Until at last we reached modern-day Kyllini, the medieval Glarenza. One hour's journey will bring me to the Frankish fortress of Clermont, the next day's objective.

■ INSPIRATION OF
THE LANDSCAPE

■ GENTLE, CLOUDY weather: I slept soundly in the humble cottage of Mrs. Nikoleta at Kyllini, beside the sea. With Fotis from Zakynthos as guide, we set out at daybreak for the fortress. The track ascends through reeds, arbutus trees, myrtle, flowering asphodel, prickly pear. And the valley, with its vineyards and olive groves, with slender, vigorous cypresses, all noble and strong, opens out as we move higher.

These Achaian and Elisian landscapes have a strange, suggestive power. Something feminine, fecund, and dangerously fascinating. They stretch out nude beneath the sun, or often beneath buoyant clouds, as languid, sportive shadows float overhead; peaceful meditations rise noiseless, tendrilous like ivy, and draw you back to the soil to take root. Peace, woman, home, child, the table spread, the bed clean, humble eternal life—all of the temptations of the feminine landscape.

Here the warrior lays his weapons involuntarily to earth, cocks his ear, listens to the gentle murmur of the olive leaves, and smiles at the world. In fury he had set forth to conquer the earth; but he was entangled by a blooming myrtle and forgot himself, delighted.

33

Likewise, one day more than seven centuries ago, the Franks appeared on this very soil. The two valiant comrades-in-arms, Geoffroy de Villehardouin and William de Champlitte set out with one hundred cavalry and a few infantrymen to conquer the Peloponnesos. They wore iron panoplies and painted shields, they carried huge lances; their Frankish steeds would neigh and, as the poet says, the Greek mares looked on longingly.

The natives, exhausted by the three besetting evils of taxes, corsairs and local tyrants, had neither strength nor inclination to resist. The one hundred iron-clad cavaliers spread terror before them; with priests leading the way, the villagers came out with incense and icons to pay tribute. They knelt down to earth, folded their hands, and begged for one thing only: that their religion be left to them, that they not be made Franks. The warriors were not in the least concerned with which road led to the heavenly kingdom—they craved only the certain earthly crown; they laughed and left the church free, as well as the priests and all their heavenly fiefs. They divided up the land among themselves, seized the cities, and built their fortresses.

Only two or three archons resisted: Leon Chamaretos at Lakedaimonia, Doxapatris Voutsaras in the stronghold of Araklovo at Skotra, and Leon Sgouros, the fearsome overlord of Corinth, Argos and Nafplio. Sgouros battled valiantly in defense of his wealth, but at the end he lost all hope, mounted his horse and flung himself unflinching from the Acrocorinthos.

Within a few months the entire Peloponnesos, with

the exception of Monemvasia, had fallen into the iron-clad Frankish embrace. They sectioned it off according to French feudal pattern; thus it was subdivided into twelve baronies with twelve principal lords, and first among them was the prince of Achaia. These twelve were followed by standard-bearers, knights and ser-geants of the Conquest. Each lord had counselors as well; when all the lords met at Andravida, the desolate village which we have already visited, the Parliament and Court were convened. And for more pressing affairs, there was a Grand Court.

Because they were but few in foreign territory, among hundreds of thousands of people of different race, dif-ferent tongue, different religion—Greeks, Slavs, Al-banians, Tzakonians, Gypsies and Jews—these formi-dable conquerors decided to remain prepared, astride their horses and armed, all year round.

But imperceptibly the feminine landscape began its intimate, gentle and noiseless encirclement. The land-scape, and the native women, wheat-brown, black-haired and wide-eyed. The blond dragons felt their re-sistance slowly disintegrating. They mingled with the women and forgot their homeland. They had children, the *Gasmouli*. The children emulated their mothers, they spoke the mother's tongue, and became Greeks. The infants' Frankish blood retreated. Acrid Greek blood, with mysterious chemical reactions, dripped into it, and the Frankish blood vanished. A new conquest began.

"Even if all the Greeks are annihilated," said Giannopoulos,[1] "and only one is left in Greece, he'll teach the barbarian conquerors Greek and make Greeks of them. The earth, the stones, the mountains are Greek and make Greeks."

"What's on your mind?" my guide Fotis asks.

"Do you know," I ask him, "who were here on this soil before the liberation of Greece?"

"Of course I know! The Turks!"

"And before the Turks?"

"The Franks."

"And what became of them all?"

"We ate them up!" cried Fotis, opening wide a gaping mouth of sharp yellow teeth. "We ate them up, boss! Too bad there aren't others!"

It was morning, we were hiking, the air was clean; Fotis' appetite had awakened; that most active verb "we ate" gave him an incredible hunger. Turks and Franks were transformed by his fancy to roasts and salads.

"And how is it that they didn't eat us?" I asked.

Fotis laughed.

"We're inedible," he said. "We've got a dog's hide. My late father used to tell a tale, I'll pass it on to you so you'll understand. He had a brother, a grocer, in a village way off in Egypt. You know, Misiri. All day long, with his apron on, he'd work, back and forth. He sold on credit to the fellahin and kept track. They'd have celebrations, *fantazies* as the fellahin call them, so they'd want butter, rice, sugar, honey, tobacco. Uncle filled their baskets, and wrote and wrote and wrote.

When the ledgers were full, he sold all the houses in the village, sold their cotton and their lands, sold their donkeys; he swallowed up the entire village. That's the way a Greek is."

We fell silent. Climbing steadily, we were now passing two files of tiny, tender-tipped cypresses. A small bird with a white breast perched on one of the tips and the entire young cypress leaned over. At that instant bells rang out from deep in a shaded ravine. All silver, brisk and joyous. Two shrill, silvery voices tittering and sporting in the ravine, like two partridges.

"What's going on, Fotis?" I asked my guide, who had taken off his cap and was frantically crossing himself.

"There's a little monastery here, the Madonna of Blachernae. Today's her grace. Listen how the priests are yelling!"

I laughed.

"D'you understand the bells?" he asked.

I shrugged my shoulders.

"Well then, I'll tell you myself. They're saying: Dong! Dong! Dong! Five drachmas on the plate, Christians! Ding! Ding! Ding! Just one drachma on the plate, Christians! Listen to what I tell you: The priests are yelling, not the Madonna."

Fotis again began to cross himself, as if shocked by his own words.

An old woman with a basket passed. She stopped and proffered us a few figs. We were refreshed. Two little girls went by on a tiny burro. Both were blond, with blue eyes.

Suddenly, at the turn of a hill, I lifted my arm joyfully. Before me, high atop the summit of the mount, the redoubtable fortress of Clermont gleamed. Square, wounded, but still erect.

Villehardouin worked on it for three years. He seized the rich incomes of the insatiable Latin clergy and transformed them into walls, gates and battlements. The Frankish priests anathematized him, but he chuckled and raised his fortress high. It had become so impregnable that even if the Franks had been expelled from everywhere else, as the chronicles relate, possession of Clermont would have enabled them to reconquer the Peloponnesos. A few years later the Franks began to mint their own coinage here, the *tournesia*, with squared crosses, fortresses and royal lilies embossed upon them.

I wish to be alone, and so bid Fotis goodbye. At the feet of the fortress lies the village, flattened in the sun. Dogs begin to bark, kerchiefed heads appear in doorways, sooty piglets, like plump rats, chase after one another, deeply engrossed. Two masons clinging to a wall stop their labors in mid-air to stare.

"Stranger?" an old man cries to me.

"Stranger!" I reply, and quicken my pace.

"Come over and have a coffee!"

But without responding, I climb on up the mount. I'm in a hurry. Conversations, treats and incessant questions are irksome when a castle stands deserted and beckoning above you.

As I passed through the narrow, open fortress gate, crossed the devastated Gothic chambers and grass-

choked courtyards, and, scaling a wild fig tree, reached
the upper level and stood atop a rock, I felt like uttering
a piercing cry, like a hawk. Sudden joy seized me. In
a flash the Franks returned to the Peloponnesos, rav-
ished it, filled it with blond-headed children and savage
fortresses, and vanished. I was delighted because for an
instant, sluggish time assumed the rhythm craved by
every impatient soul.

At my every step menacing flocks of crows soared up,
covered the sun for a moment and descended, screech-
ing, to the other edge of the fortress. On the hillside
and on the plain below the bells of invisible sheep
tinkled coolly, like water, in the heat. I stood in a Gothic
window and looked out over the plain of Glarenza, lying
so fertile and serene, and around it the shimmering sea.
Far beyond shone the divine isles: Zakynthos, Kefalonia, and just barely visible, a vision of blue light,
Ithaca.

What a shock the Franks must have been for the
Greeks, those abject serfs! Gourmands, drinkers, libertines, immobile valiants, first in battle, first in wine or
with a kiss. Frightened, still trembling, the natives would
have clustered around them, looking on with trepidation. How they would revel and feast! They brought
troubadours with them who sang of love, with strange
musical instruments! An unheard-of love, romantic,
filled with unexpected religious devotion, sensuality and
purity. New dances, new songs, a rich new vision of life,
overflowing with flesh, yet at the same time mysteriously
and unyieldingly pursuing that shining, wing-filled flesh-

less bird, the spirit. Great bodies, ample souls, thunderous laughter, free opinion and scorn of death. They dressed in variegated colors and sparkled in the sun, and charged, each with a multitude, like natural forces. Little by little the natives regained their courage and began to assume foreign traits, eating, singing and waging war like the Franks.

The serfs took heart, the flesh matured, the mind flowered. A strange romantic culture was grafted to Classical Greece. Bizarre philological fruits burst forth: *Callimachus and Chrysorrohe, Lybistrus and Rhodamne, Belthadrus and Chrysanza, Florias and Plazia Flore, Iberius and Margarona* . . .[2]

It was as if a new Euphorion, the supreme *Gasmoulos,* the erotic fruit of Faust and Helen, had been born on Greek earth. He would have had his mother's heavenly body and his father's insatiable, romantic soul, pining incurably for the boundless.

For a long time I enjoyed the serene plain of Glarenza from the Gothic window, and in my mind brought the departed Frankish shades back to life. A compelling chance to ponder amid this wreckage, with dignity and courage, that sternest aspect of life: death. But I was too late. I heard sudden steps and French conversation behind me. I turned. There were two French girls, one short-legged and enthused, the other silent. A young man with a spare, ironic face and small gray-green eyes followed them. My vision was shattered; the fortress had been violated, the Franks had come once more; I hastily withdrew from the window, clambered down the wild fig and left.

I was destined, as you will see, to encounter these three later on at a deserted Arkadian stopover and to remain together with them for a while, conversing during the voyage.

■ MEDIEVAL GLARENZA

■ WHEN I CAME down from Clermont to the valley and reached the sparse houses of Kyllini, the festival had caught fire. From all the surrounding villages men and women had come to the monastery of the Madonna of Blachernae, and now they spilled over into the seaside taverns to celebrate her grace, eating and getting drunk.

The taverns were decorated with oleanders and flags; fiddlers had arrived from Zakynthos across the way, carts were continually unloading squealing, excited women, bawling babies, colorful blankets and baskets.

Yesterday, however, this very same shore, with its fine bright sand and the scattered remains of renowned Frankish Glarenza, held an inexpressible dignity. Quiet, calm, before dawn I wandered along beside the sea and delighted to see my footprints stretch out along the sand, and then suddenly vanish. In the unearthly still of dawn the mind can enjoy unimpeded the harsh pleasures that it prefers. Ruined cities, wars, riches, commerce that has been eradicated, the toil of man founded upon air. And like a hawk the mind cries out amid the ruins, happy because it senses that it has reached the lofty point of viewing the abyss as a fatherland.

Here, six or seven centuries ago at the now decrepit harbor of Glarenza, what activity, what delights and profits! Ships set sail hence for Venice, Ancona, Durazzo, Alexandria, laden with silks, raisins, acorns, figs, honey, oil, wax. . . . Here, in the now invisible palace, the Grand Court of Achaia gathered to decide on war or peace, or princely marriages. Here in Glarenza the Court of the Bourgeoisie, of the townsmen, convened to arbitrate the quarrels of the natives, or those between Franks and natives. And in this toppled Gothic church Franciscan monks from Assisi intoned their vespers, and gazed through the slitlike windows at the cool and enduring sea. When the first of the Villehardouins died, he who had so loved Glarenza, on this very shore the dirge which the chronicle relates would have broken out:

Great mourning spread throughout the Morea,
for he was held in high esteem, and much beloved
for his benign dominion, and the wisdom that he
     showed.[1]

Lament, voices and men vanished like reeds, like the rustle of the reeds. But suddenly, today at the festival the sand shifted once more, among the rocks and trees indefatigable men appeared, continually defeated, falling and then reappearing from the earth. They seemed full of humor, revitalized, without memory. Staring about them in the thickly populated atmosphere of Glarenza, they remembered nothing. So they find a place in the taverns, sip wine, eat meat and begin the dance. The shore fills with life anew. Peddlers come, hawking *pasteli*, pistachios, *passa-tempo* and peaches. One salesman screeches in a shrill, repugnant voice: "Icons, incense, dream books, songs, romances!"

The women are yellowed, the children walk about with huge bloated bellies; here malaria has forced the race to its knees. This is one of the bitterest of sights: to see, as you tour the Peloponnesos, your race being reduced by the fever. Most of the Greeks are sullen, lacking appetite, with neither physical nor spiritual fortitude, without eagerness for a single idea, because the fever is devouring them. They must drink, intoxicate themselves, something exceptional must happen—a festival or a wedding—in order for them to loosen their lips a little and smile.

Malaria, the Turkish yoke, primitivity—all of these have stifled our laughter. The body has neither strength nor good humor, primitive nightmares still oppress us, the mind has not become civilized, has not been put at ease, has not yet learned to play. We Greeks are here passing through a disagreeable transitory period. We are no longer slaves, but we are not yet free men.

The revelers at today's festival shout, moan and sing, aroused by the wine. Just like the clever demon of the tale who unroofed all the houses so that all their secrets showed, so here the wine lays bare all of man's hidden parts. Shouts, songs, dances, fights, teasing, flirtations— but not for an instant did I hear a genuine laugh, unadulterated and without malice. I did not see a single person gaze at those throngs of celebrating men and women, or at the sea, or at the glass of wine he was drinking, and laugh—from overabundance of heart alone. They laugh because someone has slipped and fallen, because one has cut another to the quick, or because someone attempts something he can't manage.

Only one old man, Barba-Thanases, was laughing guilelessly because his heart overflowed. He must have been seventy years old, from a village near Kavasilas. He was ruddy, his gray eyes were without lashes, his mustache was twirled. He watched the young men and women dancing and couldn't sit still; he leaped up, minced about on wobbly, ramshackle knees, his eyes streamed and his cracked voice began an *amané*. An *amané* of misery, all falsetto and passion. And afterward he fell exhausted back into his chair.

I sat down beside him to admire him. In my life I've seen several such old men who loved life and frantically bid it goodbye. One, most of all, in a Cretan mountain village. Old Perdikokostandi. He could see no longer, but his ears were alert, he would sit on his doorstep and listen to the passersby. And when he heard a youthful woman's voice, a young girl going to the fountain, he started up, stretching out his hands:

"Come here, my dear child, and let me touch you!" he called out entreatingly as he searched the air.

And sometimes the girls that knew him would feel pity for him and go over. And then, old Perdikokostandi would insatiably spread his shriveled palm over the youngster's face; he would caress it with his finger tips, slowly, slowly, from the forehead to the eyes, the nose, the lips, the chin; then the palm would ascend again, deliberate and famished. Then his eyes would begin to trickle.

"Hey, don't cry, granddad!" the girls would tell him, laughing. "Why're you crying?"

"And why shouldn't I cry, my child, when at last I'm dying and leaving behind me a world filled with such young maidens!"

Such was Barba-Thanases here at Glarenza.

"I'm a Lothario!" he cried. "I'm seventy and the girls still love me. Why? Why, you'll ask? Because I'm a great lover and the women know it."

But old Marketos, the tramp, who was seated near him at the same table, tossed his head with scorn. He was a fearsome Kefalonian, one-eyed, with a crippled right arm and an immense forehead. His rags stank of tobacco and deep sweat. To his crippled arm he had fitted a piece of iron, bent like a hook, and with it he snatched scraps of bread, meat and fruit from the tables.

He rolled his huge, brimming eye and stared at me:

"C'mon," he said, "let me stand you a drink. They call me Marketos."

"I'll treat, Barba-Marketos," I said. "Let's call over Barba-Thanases too."

"Let him be, we don't need him!" said the savage Kefalonian, contorting his mouth with disgust. "He's always drooling over women. Has he no shame? Why, with women I'd . . . Give me half a cigarette and I'll show you."

I handed him the cigarette; he put it in his mouth, puffed it, made a pfft! and flung it away.

"Pfft!" he shouted again. "That's how I rate women. Nothing! One snort of tobacco. And you know why? 'Cause I've known a few in my lifetime, curse 'em. That lout you're looking at, Barba-Thanases, is all talk. Leave him be, listen to me!"

A weird envy had brightened his circular Cyclopean eye. Everyone was paying court to old Thanases, treating and teasing him. No one turned to look at him, the Kefalonian with the wild, widely traveled soul.

"Listen to me," he repeated and hooked my knee. "I've traveled, I've seen and suffered a lot; I've been starving, robbed, I've killed, been thrown in jail, dug a tunnel and cleared out! You listen to me! That blabbermouth hasn't budged from the village, he's a homebody, a raisin grower, has a house and children. Devil take him!"

He spoke and spat on the floor, as if describing to me the most loathsome thing on earth.

"Don't be misled because I've got one eye. He who has but one eye sees better than he with two. Because he knows what 'eye' means. And he who has none at all sees everything. You listen to me— Dry up, Barba Thanases. We've had enough of your chatter. Sit down, drink!"

He grabbed his glass and tossed it down. Then he turned to old Thanases:

"Hey, you, aren't you ashamed? You're a man, are you? Men don't talk about women, and you ought to know it!"

Poor old Barba-Thanases shrank back.

"They talk of brave deeds, of thievery, murder and

voyages," continued Barba-Marketos, and his forehead shot off sparks. "Once, when I was in Stamboul—"

"Oho! The same thing all over again!" shouted Barba-Thanases in despair. "We know it alright! The pasha, the graveyard, the golden chain—"

"The gentleman, however, doesn't know it. We've heard you out. Now he'll listen to me, to see just who is who. Pay attention, Mr.— your name, please?"

"Spinoza."

I recalled years past when I had cards printed "Nicholas Spinoza, professor," and whenever I traveled I passed them out to whoever asked my name.

"Listen then, Mr. Spinoza . . ."

And he began to relate a fantastic, lively yarn: How he had served on a ship, been seized by corsairs and taken away to the City, dragged to a cemetery and lowered into a tomb, where, those very days, a pasha had been interred, and how he had taken the golden chain . . .

An amazing vision, with the minutest of details, with tightly drawn plot, like one of Stevenson's tales of far-away, brightly lit islands, in a dream atmosphere where miracles walk the streets like the simplest everyday acts. I can no longer recall it to tell, but the color, the accuracy of description, the bas-relief decoration, the bastions of the City, its mosques, the Oriental night, and the greenish bloated corpse of the pasha lying face up with the heavy golden chain across his belly have all remained, full of fascination, in my memory.

With the exception of Panait Istrati,[2] I have never

heard anyone narrate with such descriptive power. However, on my Peloponnesian tour, as you will see, it was in store for me to hear a third, another old man, a priest from the region of Trebizond whom I met at Mistra.

The heat was cloudy, stifling. Old Marketos was still telling his story, the air reeked of retsina and fumes from roasting meat. A cart passed, piled high with watermelon. Everyone dashed off and shortly returned, each embracing a plump watermelon. The melons were sliced open, the air took on the smell of sea, throats were refreshed. Old Marketos plunged his face into half a melon, ate the seed-filled red flesh with relish and fell silent.

The soul was calmed, the body soothed, a single fruit changed the world. Then—as though everything in this world happens with some coherence—a slender, amicable musician appeared and halted before our table. His eyes were blue-green, his fingers long and slender. He sat down, gently removed his *santouri* from its red bag, set it upon his knees, stroking it lightly with his hand, and began to play and sing. *Amanés*, Oriental passion, monotonous primeval cravings, those same ones that return again and again, doleful and sluggish, to suck at man's brain. The soul's foundations are unsettled, you are overcome by a lethargic swoon, your heart becomes an overripe fruit. The revelers round about fell into sudden torpor, their sharp and rapacious eyes dimmed; beneath the restless, cunning Greek appeared the languorous Oriental.

The *santouri* player finished and mopped his sweat;

his gaze, which had left us, returned to look us over. He took a cup from his pocket, collected a few small coins, and folded his hands to rest. It pleased me; so I started to talk with him.

"How did you learn *santouri?*" I asked.

"I was twenty. I heard the *santouri* at a festival. It took my breath away. For three days I couldn't eat.

" 'What's the matter with you?' my father asked me.

" 'I want to learn *santouri!*'

" 'Have you no shame, fellow?'

" 'I want to learn *santouri.*'

"I'd scraped some money together so I could get married when the time came. I spent it and bought a *santouri*. Here, the very one you're looking at. Taking it with me, I left for Patra and found the late Kostaki, the *santouri* teacher. I fell down at his feet.

" 'What d'you want, young fellow?' he asked me.

" 'I want to learn *santouri.*'

" 'Eh, and why d'you fall down at my feet?'

" 'I've got no money to pay you.'

" 'All right, stay on, I've no need of payment.'

"I stayed with him for a year and learned. And now I wander here and there, to festivals and weddings, and earn my bread. Humans be blessed. When I'm playing they'll speak to me but I don't hear. Sometimes, though, I hear, but I can't answer. I want to, but I can't."

"But why?"

"Eh! Passion!"

"Do you play at home?"

"How could I play there, my man! At home I've got bothers; wife, children, what'll we eat—worries! The *santouri* needs a pure heart. As soon as my wife says a needless word, what sort of heart do you expect me to have for the *santouri?* If the children are hungry, what sort of disposition for playing? The *santouri* wants you to think only about *santouri!*"

Never had I heard the essence and the rapture of art more simply and perfectly defined. Only at the instant when you can free yourself from the loom of necessity do you sense what man's pure, selfless shout means— song! The ragged *santouri* player, following his heart, had reached the peak of aesthetic truth.

I went down to the sea, to the timeless element of Greece, swam, stretched out on the rocks listening to the distant hum of the human flock, and gazed far out toward Zakynthos, and farther still, toward our mystical homeland, Ithaca.

And suddenly the ship of Odysseus sprang up once again from the eternal sea, riding over the waves. Astride the tiller as is his custom sits the captain, with his pointed cap pulled down to his eyebrows. His cunning little eyes sparkle, his brows meshed—as if weighing with his eye an island that he feels like seizing, or a cloud which has suddenly appeared in the sky, puffed out with wind, or his strength and the powers of the immortals, before deciding if it best profits him to appear courageous or cunning.

I look away toward Ithaca, and on my forehead I

sense the cool breeze that blew across his temples when at daybreak he opened the palace gate—his wife, his son, his homeland, his gods could contain him no longer—and leaped aboard his ship to leave.

He took to the sea and never turned back. Someone said: "I saw him talking secretly with Helen one evening among the canebrakes of the Eurotas." Another: "I saw him passing the Pillars of Hercules and leaving the world behind." And one night, Telemachus caught sight of him in his sleep: ascending, ascending Olympus, carrying the oars high on his shoulders, like two wings. Telemachus leaped up terrified from his bed crying: "My father is dead."

But you, ship's master of Greece, with the pointed cap, the cunning, sober eye, with the mind that creates myths and rejoices in a lie as a work of art, you stand, stubborn, courageous and crafty, aboard Greece's vessel, and unsleeping, grip the rudder.

The sun was sinking, the sea had become like wine, the songs of the populace turned wilder, pipes began to shrill again. Two or three carts passed by at water's edge filled with women who fell shrieking and laughing into one another's embrace. The festival closed down. And I, squatting now on the pebbles, folded my arms like a laborer. In my mind I held a rich reward, my day's wage: the indomitable fortress, the colorful festival, and finally at nightfall, atop the waves, the great Shade.

■ LANDSCAPE OF
OLYMPIA

■ Buzzers, noisemakers, violins; men and women are howling, children bawling; crows squawk and horses neigh; flocks of pigs grunt, rooting in the river mud, and others, slung roasted over shoulders, protrude their incredible pointed snouts, browned and shiny, from the bag, as we might see them on ancient vases. Dust and nauseating smoke from stuffed intestines revolving over the coals rise in the heat. The whole riverbank hums, teeming with men and animals, and the multicolored blankets, bags, portable stoves and filth gleam in the fearful sun. The entire sacred Classical region of the Kladeos opened out before us like a motley, exotic Gypsy encampment.

Olympia. Contests, gleaming, exercised bodies, wreathed and immortal athletes, Pindarian verses, gods, heroes, pediments; the entire ancient marbled vision swayed for an instant, defiled by the sweating, shouting celebrators given over to their trade. Books and schoolmasters have led us astray, ancient Greece has been reduced in our imagination to a series of soulless marble statues; and when we visit the ancient ruins as pilgrims, we like to see them empty and silent, in romantic desertion.

53

But ancient Greece was full of shouts, brawls and merchants; during the great games, just as today, the Kladeos and Alpheos roared with humans, horses and pigs. The patchwork huts would have been flung up in the same way then, and meats, dried seeds, toys and clay gods would have been sold. Ancient Greece was not a supernatural bloom, odorless and untouched; it was a tree which took root deep in the earth, devoured mud and flowered. Indeed, the more mud it consumed, the richer its blossoms developed. Renowned ancient simplicity, equilibrium and serenity were not the natural, effortless virtues of a calm and balanced race; they were trying ordeals, the booty of fierce struggle; for centuries the dark, orgiastic powers of earth grappled with the enlightened powers of man. And it happened—that is the Greek miracle—that for some years human reason triumphed over the chaos.

I climb slowly up from the station and pass through the little hamlet, by the coffeehouses, fruit markets and grocery stores, beholding the living descendants with their ugly, twisted bodies and cunning little eyes. Another time, perhaps, I would have been gripped by useless anger or romantic melancholy, because I would have compared these woebegone bodies with the statues. But now I realize that the forebears would have been the same, and that only through struggle and selection would some few bodies achieve the lofty victory of the flower. And then the artist would come to render them immortal. The countless other bodies which could not win fell back, mud into mud, and became roots, nourishing the bloom.

I was pleased to have avoided both anger and melancholy, and I turned to the ragged, barefoot youth carrying my bag. He was an appealing sort, eyes large as if entranced, hanging lips; when I gave him my bag, the rabble at the station jeered me.

"You're giving it to him? Why he's a moron! Yah yah yah, Mitro!"

But Mitro smiled, and his wide, gleaming white teeth showed.

"Don't listen to them, boss," he said, to reassure me. "Don't listen. I'm a good man, that's why they call me an idiot."

Caravans of tourists were making their way up the dusty road. The sky had a harsh metallic tint, like steel. Automobiles, carts, donkeys, dogs were yapping; it was midday. From the shade of an olive tree a cow turned its large velvet eyes upon us and stared with profound indifference.

I took a path beneath thick pines and climbed up to the Kronion to view the sacred landscape from the height. Nobility and calm meditation, the smiling valley among low, placid mountains, protected from the savage north wind and from the hot south wind, open only toward the west, the sea, whence the moist sea breeze blows, flowing up the course of the Alpheos. In all Greece there is no landscape more inspiring, none that so gently and perseveringly incites peace and reconciliation. The ancients chose it with unerring eye, so that every four years all the races of Greece might gather here, to sport and to fraternize.

Greece was racked by jealousy, enmity, civil war; democracies, aristocracies and tyrannies were annihilating one another; enclosed valleys, isolated islands, secluded shores and small independent city-states formed a unique, many-headed organism, each part of which despised the other; passions seethed in every breast. Suddenly, though, in the summer of every fourth year, wreathed heralds, the *spondoforoi*, set out from this sacred vale, running to Hellenism's farthest reaches to proclaim the *hieromynia*, the armistice of the games, summoning friend and foe to Olympia to play. From the entire Peloponnesos and central Greece, from Macedonia, Thessaly, Epiros and Thrace, from the Black Sea shores, Asia Minor and Egypt, Cyrene, Magna Graeca and Sicily, athletes and pilgrims hastened to the pan-Hellenic cradle of sport. Slaves could not set foot here, nor could criminals nor barbarians, nor women. Only free Greeks.

No other people has so perfectly comprehended the hidden and the visible value of the game. When, through daily struggle, life succeeds in overcoming the enemies around it—natural forces, wild beasts, hunger, thirst and sickness—sometimes it chances to have some strength remaining. It seeks to expend this strength in play. At the moment that the game begins, civilization begins. As long as life struggles to endure, to protect itself from its enemies, to sustain itself on earth's crust, civilization cannot emerge. It is born in the instant that life fulfills its immediate needs and begins to enjoy a little relief.

How shall this relief be put to use, how can it be divided among the various social levels, how can it be increased and ennobled as much as possible? From the solution that each race and epoch gives to these problems, the value and essence of their culture can be judged.

I wander to and fro among the ruins of Altis, seeing once again with delight the fossil-bearing stones from which the temples were built. The Christians shattered them, earthquakes have toppled them, rains and the flooding of the Alpheos have washed away their vivid coloring. The statues were burned, turned to lime; few have been left to us, but still they are enough to console our minds. I gather two or three sprigs of savory that have taken root in the hollow where Phideas' chryselephantine statue is said to have stood, and their timeless fragrance covers my fingers.

Here, long before men, the gods had grappled in this mystical arena. Zeus struggled with his father Kronos to wrest his kingdom from him; Apollo, the god of light, defeated Hermes at running and Ares at hand-to-hand combat. The mind overcame time, the light triumphed over the dark powers of intrigue and violence. Later, after the gods, the heroes joined combat here; Pelops from Asia defeated bloodthirsty, barbaric Oenomaos and took his daughter, the horse-taming Hippodameia. The advanced, serene and graceful culture of Ionia subdued the uncouth natives, mastered horses, made fast man's power. Another hero, Herakles, after clearing the Augeian stables, came here and offered up great sacrifices to the new god, Zeus; and with the ashes which remained from the burned slaughter, he erected an altar and proclaimed the first Olympic games. With fresh ashes from the sacrifices the sacred altar rose continually higher; Olympia became the great forge where the races of Greece hammered out their bronzed bodies.

Not solely to make those bodies handsome. Never did the Greeks pursue art for its own sake; beauty's mission was always the service of life. The ancients wanted their bodies strong and handsome so that they might accept a strong and balanced mind. And still more—the loftiest aim—to be able to defend their city.

For the Greeks gymnastics were an essential preparation for the social life of the citizen. The perfect citizen was he who could, by frequenting gymnasium and arena, work his body, make it both powerful and harmonic, that is to say handsome, and have it ready to defend his race. Look at a statue of the Classical period and you will understand instantly whether the man it depicts is free or slave; he is revealed by his body. Handsome athletic frame, calm stance, discipline of passion: these are the characteristics of the free man. The slave is invariably depicted as flabby or sickly, with abrupt, uncontrolled movements. Dionysos, god of drink, stands serene; his inferiors, the slaves, the Selenoi and satyrs, romp and tumble indecently around him, dead drunk.

Harmony of mind and body—behold the lofty ideal of the Greek. Overdevelopment of one at the expense of the other was considered barbaric. When the Greeks began to decline, the body of the athlete began to overdevelop and destroy his spirit. Euripides was one of the first to protest and to proclaim the danger to the spirit at the hands of athleticism. Galen later complained: "They eat, they drink, they sleep and empty their bellies, they roll in the mud and dust—that's the life the athletes lead!" The great martyr Herakles, who in his years of glory strode from labor to labor perfectly balancing mind and body, little by little acquired a huge body, a narrow forehead, became a tippler and a glutton. Artists who had created the ideal figure of youth in the great epochs now depicted the athletic bodies which they observed about them with raw realism, weighty and barbarous.

In Greece, as everywhere, when realism finally begins to reign, civilization declines. Thus we reached the unbelieving, realistic, bombastic Hellenistic epoch, with no ideal beyond that of the individual. From chaos to the Parthenon, and now from the Parthenon back to chaos. The great, merciless rhythm. Sentiments and passions burst out, free man loses his discipline, the halter which held his instincts in rigid balance escapes his hands. Passions, sentimentalism, realism; mystic, melancholy craving floods the face; fearful mythological visions become ornaments; Aphrodite is stripped naked like an ordinary woman; Zeus becomes a stylish rogue, and Herakles reverts to the beast. Following the Peloponnesian Wars, Greece begins to dissolve, faith in the homeland vanishes, individualism triumphs. No longer is the god or the idealized youth the protagonist, but rather the wealthy townsman with his sensual pleas-

ures and affectations, skeptical, materialistic, a rake.
Talent has taken the place of genius, and now "good
taste" replaces talent. Art fills with children and co-
quettish women, realistic scenes, beastly men or schoolmasters. . . .

The sun had set, shadows spread out over the ruins.
Tourists come and go, guidebooks in hand, wandering
through the Gymnasium to the Palestra, the Rectory,
the Heraion, the Treasuries, clambering at last over the
temple of Zeus. They've sweated in the attempt to re-
create the ancient spectacle, the naked youths, the pur-
ple-clad judges, the sporting events, the shouts of the
crowd, the lad with a golden sickle who cuts the seventeen *thalloi*, the sacred branches of the wild olive, from
which the seventeen victors' wreaths would be plaited.
The clamoring spectators would pelt them with apples,
pomegranates and flowers, while others would even toss
belts, parasols and tunics. And on the far bank of the
Alpheos the women cheered as well, acclaiming the victors.

Some of the local peasants broke away from the festival to come and see why so many "lords" have hurried
here and what they can be looking at. A soldier guides
them, explaining. Here they played football, here the
discus, here's where their priests lived, here were the
statues. The Germans made the diggings

"And do you know what they discovered? Treasure!
Listen, listen!"

He leafed through some papers he held.

"A hundred and thirty marble statues and reliefs, thirteen thousand brass objects, six thousand coins, four hundred inscriptions, a thousand items of pottery, forty monuments!"

"And gold? Gold?" screeched a peasant, and his eyes bulged.

"It doesn't say," the soldier replied. "The excavations lasted six years. Three hundred were at work."

"Did they spend a lot?"

"Millions!" sighed the soldier.

The peasants gape, they move past the spot where I was stretched out on a rock in Phideas' workshop. An old man comes over to me.

"Tell me, you ought to know, why'd the Germans go to such expense? I don't understand it. Where's the profit?"

"Scientific," I answered, bored.

"I don't understand it. They've stolen the statues and sold them, I tell you."

"They worked for science. . . ."

"I don't understand, I tell you. They must have stolen them."

"They worked for glory, not profit. Can't you understand that?"

"I don't understand," the modern Greek replied.

Another group passed. A fat housewife's eyes stared wide.

"How could they carry such huge boulders? Unbelievable!"

"Not at all unbelievable," answered an emaciated

oldster wearing a fustanella. "They didn't carry them."

"Then who did?" the woman asked uneasily.

"The gods moved them. In those days they'd help men. Now, why would they want to help us! We're unbelievers, what do you expect!"

Everyone was satisfied with this explanation. I too was satisfied, perfectly. A little altered, the answer of the old kilt-wearer explains all man's miracles. It suffices to give the word "god" the profound human meaning that, analogous with every era, becomes it.

■ THE SYMBOLIC
ATMOSPHERE OF MYTH

■ TODAY THE weather is cooler. About midnight a fierce storm had broken out; the merry-makers who were sleeping in the open leaped up, you could hear them howling amid the thunderclaps and whipping rain. The old Olympian god was toying with his worshipers; in daylight he was Zeus Agoraios, supervising commerce so that blankets and brassware and horses and pigs would sell well; but last night he had secretly rounded up the clouds, to see the mortals sopped and shrieking, and to pass his time. Zeus became Jupiter Pluvius and came down to earth. He thundered in order to terrify them, and flung bolt after bolt of lightning to make them out in the darkness. He was amusing himself. And in the morning he drove the clouds away, the sky laughed, spotlessly clean, and Zeus, grinning slyly, invisible, took a seat once more, Agoraios, in the midst of the fair with weighted scale in hand.

The Kronion gleamed, drenched, in the sun. The pines were fragrant, the dust had settled, the air had an inexpressible softness and sweetness. The body rejoices, strolling freely and contented, as though it were a lump of earth which thirsted, and has now drunk and been refreshed. The ancient marble is cleansed and rinsed, and smiles as though it were not in ruins. How the statues of gods and men would have shone, how they would have twinkled in the leafy verdure of Olympia after such a rain! But the Christians smashed them, earthquakes have toppled them, fire has transformed them to lime dust. Chronos-Kronos bore them, and Chronos-Kronos has ravenously devoured them. Now on the earthen table of the father only a few legs and heads remain strewn about, leavings from the horrible feast.

I climb the low hill to the museum, hurrying to see the two superb remaining pediments, and the labors of Herakles, and the Hermes of Praxiteles. I'm hurrying, as though afraid that these survivals too will be swallowed up by earth. Reflect that man's noble striving transgresses inhuman, eternal laws. Thus our lives and efforts gain a heroic and tragic intensity. We have no more than a single instant at our disposal; let us make eternity of that instant—there is no other immortality.

When I came face to face with the main hall of the museum, my heart revived. Serenely illuminated by the morning light, they still live: the centaurs, the Lapithae, Apollo, Herakles, Nike. I was delighted. This world is guided by extrahuman laws; we sense that from moment to moment, in this fateful hour in which it is our lot to live, a bomb might fall and turn man's most precious achievements to ashes. When we enjoy a work of art, our pleasure is tightly interwoven with the danger of eternal separation hanging above it.

As you gaze at these two great pediments, you sense

how correctly a Far Eastern sage defined the purpose of art: "Art is not in depicting the body—rather the forces that shape the body." Here, primarily in the west pediment, these creative forces seethe visibly beneath the translucent skin. The symposium has come to an end, the centaurs have gotten drunk and rushed to grab the Lapithaean women. A centaur flings out his leg and embraces a woman, and at the same time squeezes her breast with his gross hand. The woman appears to have fainted from the pain, and from some mysterious, ineffable pleasure. Elsewhere the strugglers bite and stab at one another, the beast is set loose, wild orgasm explodes, primeval scenes of human against ape men are revived before us. A strange calm, however, pervades all this incredible, primordial passion: because, serene in the midst of the frenzied mortals, unseen by the combatants, extending simply his right arm, stands Apollo.

The master who created this great vision just a few years before the Parthenon had surpassed the virginal awkwardness of the ancient artisan, but had not yet achieved the perfection of the classic instant. He was still engaged in the assault, smoldering with passion and impatience for victory, and had not yet touched the summit. He had upset one balance, but had not quite reached the other; he rushed, steaming and all impetuous, toward his goal. And if this pediment moves us so profoundly, it is because it has not yet reached man's peak. Perfection. You can still discern the hero suffering and struggling.

And another delight: On this pediment you can observe the entire breadth of the hierarchy: god, free man, woman, slave and beast. The god stands at the center, erect, calm, master of his strength. He sees the horror but is not distraught; he subdues rage and passion, but without becoming indifferent, because he calmly extends his arm, bestowing victory upon him whom he prefers. The Lapithae, the men, hold fast the stamp of humanity on their faces to the limit of their ability; they neither howl nor are seized by panic; nevertheless they are men, not gods; a wrinkle of their brow and a slight tremor on their lips indicates that they are suffering. The women suffer even more, but a dark pleasure is indistinguishably mingled with their pain, as if even against their will they enjoyed being seized by terrible masculine characters and shedding blood for their favor. The slaves recline with familiarity, without restraint, looking on. In the period in which this pediment was created, these reclining forms at the edges could not have depicted gods; gods would never have lolled about this way, forgetting their sacred dignity. Finally the centaurs, licentious and drunken beasts, fall upon women and boys, howling and gnashing; no mind exists to give order to power, to give nobility to passion.

This is a superb moment, where all of the graduated levels of existence retain their character so completely. In this marble instant all characteristics coexist: divine imperturbability, free man's discipline, the outburst of the beast, the realistic representation of the slave. After a few generations, the latter two elements will reign; realistic passion will spread, deforming both men and gods; the bridle will be loosed and art will degenerate, rampaging. From the dynamic tragedy of this Olympian pediment, and from the holy serenity of the Parthenon, we shall come to the unbridled verbalism of Pergamon.

Upon this pediment you rejoice to see all the seeds of development, fulfillment and decadence existing simultaneously, in one flash of synthesis. Perfection is a difficult, dangerous and momentary balance above chaos; throw a little weight either to the right or the left and it will topple.

The pediment gives us still another pleasure. We gaze at it and reflect: this pediment came about just after the Greeks had defeated the Persians, and a joyful swell of relief, pride and strength swept over Greece. Greece sensed her power, the world within and around her was revitalized, gods and men were illuminated by a new light—everything must be renewed, temples, statues, paintings, poetry. An eternal commemoration of the victories of the Greeks over the barbarians must be erected. How could that commemoration be achieved by sculpture?

The great artist glimpses timeless, changeless symbols beneath the flow of everyday reality. Behind the spasmodic, often incoherent actions of mortal men he views clearly the great currents that sweep souls along. He transposes ephemeral events into immortal air. A great master regards realistic depiction as a deformation, a caricature of the eternal.

That is why Classical Greece's great masters—and not only the sculptors—desiring to render contemporary triumphs eternal, transposed history high up into the symbolic atmosphere of mythology. Instead of depicting their fellow Greeks battling the Persians, they brought in the Lapithae and centaurs. And beyond the Lapithae and centaurs we discern the two great, timeless adversaries: mind and beast, civilization and barbarism. Thus a historical event which occurred at one definite moment escaped time, became bound up with the entire race and with its archetypal visions; finally it escaped the race as well, and became an immortal commemoration. Thus, through this symbolic refinement, the victories of the Greeks were elevated to victories for all humanity.

The same is true of the twelve metopes which adorned the temple of Zeus, depicting the twelve labors of Herakles. Fragmented, devastated, what emotion they give us just as they have been preserved and hung here on the museum walls, to what pride they elevate our mind! How Athena, human intellect, tiny still but full of vigor, stands by and helps the athlete! In such a way, just yesterday it seems, she would have leaped from the Acropolis to aid the Greeks at Marathon and Salamis. Further along, seated upon a rock, slightly weary from the struggle but proud, how she gazes at the victorious athlete returning to offer his plunder, the Stymphalian fowl! And a little beyond, erect behind him, with what tenderness she raises her arm, and helps him to endure the weight of the earth!

From his contemporary Greeks, whom the artist cer-

tainly desired to extol, the acclaim is piously transposed
to the great forebear, the leader of the race, Herakles.
As if to say: We did not win, not this generation; the
demon of the race was the victor. The unyielding, un-
hesitating forebear-athlete triumphed. And the acclama-
tion, expressed symbolically as it is, spreads out even farther, to embrace the entire race of free men. We were
not the victors, not our race alone; man has won out,
battling to overcome wild beasts, barbarians and death,
advancing from ordeal to ordeal.

I came out onto the museum's threshold and advanced a little onto the terrace below a pine tree. Midday; the sun was boiling, and the din of the fair, like the
distant hum of bees, could be heard from the Kladeos.
Blankets were spread out on the ground for sale, green,
yellow, purple. Copper utensils shone in the sun, the
noisy, merchandise-crammed huts stretched out like a
tiny, ephemeral city. Peasants, Gypsies, fiddlers, peanut
peddlers; the cookeries smoked like altars, men and filth
were decomposed by sun; an unbearable stench rose up
even here and blended with the honeyed aroma of the
pines.

Sudden bitterness overcame me. Will we, I wonder,
ever achieve our own balance, and the calm, heroic inspiration of ancient Greece? Every pilgrim, when he ex-
tracts himself from the Olympian vision and emerges
on the museum threshold to meet the contemporary
sun, surely will put this basic question to himself with
anguish. But for us, as Greeks, the bitterness is twofold,

because we consider ourselves their descendants, and whether or not we like it, we confront ourselves with the duty of overtaking our great predecessors. And still more: the duty of every son to surpass his parents.

I struggled to find some meaning amid the festivities and the shouting, the accursed thirst for profit, the tambourines and *amanés*, among the barbershops, the cookeries and the filth. I shall imagine that all of this is the muddy root of some unsprouted future flower. And in the midst of the beastliness and rapacity I shall station an invisible god, one that will extend his arm and give nobility to the chaos.

■ KARYTAINA,
THE GREEK TOLEDO

■ THESE THREE days, from Olympia to the temple of Apollo at Bassae, from the temple to Andritsaina, and from Andritsaina to Karytaina and Megalopolis, gleam in my memory like three deep-green plane trees.

I rejoiced at the greenery, the water, the quiet canyons, the smell of sage, the cheerful, undulating mountains—the timeless Greek landscape, cut to the measure of man, flooded with light. At each instant it is slightly altered, even while remaining the same; it shimmers, flourishing its beauty, regenerates itself, and so does not tire you. It has a deep unity, and at the same time, a ceaselessly renewed variety.

Does the same rhythm not govern ancient Greek art, which was born looking at, loving and sensing this eternal landscape? Look at a work of sculpture from the great Classical period: It is not motionless, but pervaded by an indefinable shiver of life; it quivers like the wing of a hawk paused at the peak of the wind, appearing to us motionless. But a trained eye discerns that the statue continues a prior movement, one which reigned supreme in the works of the preceding generation, and

71

simultaneously lightly indicates the form that future works will take. The statue lives, moves, carries on the tradition, prepares for the future with disciplined daring, and for an instant balances the tripartite current of time.

The ancients did not admire abrupt originality; they devotedly accepted tradition, surpassing it as they carried it on. If a creative man discovered a technical solution, a new stance, a new smile, all would welcome this new asset as common property; they used it without protestations from the discoverer, trying only to develop it as much as they could through the application of their own spirit. Art then was not a personal affair, it belonged to the whole; the artist was representative of his city-state and of his race, and his goal was the immortalization of that great moment when totality endured. The artist had the closest, most immediate contacts with his people; he had but one ambition: to be able to express the desires, hopes and needs of the populace. And as the populace carries on the tradition of the preceding generation, so also the artist accepts past art as his paternal heritage and toils to advance it.

Surely the ancient artists derived this lofty teaching of obedience and daring from the Greek landscape, which faithfully sustains its unity and simultaneously is endlessly regenerated.

I walk along beneath the plane trees, stride past springs, part the willow branches in order to pass, and come upon another grove of plane trees rustling on the riverbank. The changing landscape seems like music to

me, a melody returning again and again to the same
motif. Here and there, like water flowing down the
rocks, a flock rushes down the hillsides. Or perhaps a
shepherd boy appears among the scrub oak, sun-black-
ened, frightened and satanical, with ears alert, with
thick lips. You want to stretch out your hand, plunge
it into his greasy hair and find the two tiny goat horns
that are surely hidden there. At other times you encounter peasants in your path, the sun dims and your heart
tightens. Because most of the peasants you meet are
withered and morose.

"Why are they yellow?" I ask Nikola, the guide.

"Malaria."

We take the upgrade, the rocks steam in sun; I gather
some large mauve flowers, like wild lilies. I showed them
to Nikola:

"What're these flowers called?"

And Nikola, not glancing at me, answered with con-
ceit: "*Ia!*"

He had taken me for a foreigner; having learned some
Classical Greek words in primary school, he now proffered them at every turn in order to prove to me that he
was an ancient Greek. Another grave malady, this; other
fevers. Malaria and megalomania.

I was startled. I looked at the mule driver as he
walked ahead, so haughty about his ancestry, a rag-
picker with a long, thin neck. I was startled because I
recalled the last two grandchildren of Goethe, those
wretched, incompetent, megalomaniacal brothers Maxi-
milian and Walter. The first, imagining himself a great

poet, published verses with his weighty name, Goethe. He became a laughingstock. And his brother as well, who considered himself a great musician. He too became a laughingstock. He sank into isolation, a misanthrope fanatically preparing for death. He believed himself continually in his death agony. Even in the heart of summer he would bundle up with quilts and blankets, shivering. Certainly he too suffered from malaria and megalomania.

Nikola stopped at a turn of the trail. He lifted his arm:

"The columns!" he cried, and stretched his immense neck upward.

I hurried on impatient. I knew that this was one of Greece's most brilliant temples, a work of Iktinos, erected after the great triumph of the Parthenon. Here, in these mountains, the Phigaleians had sought refuge. Escaping the plague, they erected this temple to give thanks to Apollo Epicureios.

From afar, in the opening between two hills, I could make out one corner of the temple amid the greenery. The columns were of milky stone; the surrounding emptiness was boundless, neither bird nor shepherd nor water. Blocking the distant southern horizon the Taygetos shimmered faintly, light blue, serene and omnipotent.

Only with difficulty can I sense the ancient temples; at first contact I am totally unmoved. Some length of time must pass, I must reflect intently, exercise my eye, in order to appreciate the simplicity and wisdom, the power and grace of an ancient temple. And here, a long

time elapsed before I could discover the profound correspondence of landscape and temple. Slowly, with
practice, the temple appeared to me as a segment of
the mountain, distinctively situated among the other
mountains, from the same stone, and of the same
rhythm; and only by gazing at these stones did I sense
that they were fashioned and located in such a way as
to express the essence of all the surrounding mountain
waste. It resembles the head of the landscape, the sacred
enclosure where its mind gleams. Here ancient art does
not surprise you; it elevates you gently, by way of a human path, so that you are not out of breath at the summit.

An old woman emerged from the nearby caretaker's
hut. In her hand she held two figs and a bunch of
grapes—the first to ripen on that high plateau. A sweet,
slender, affable old woman who certainly would have
sparkled in her youth.

"What's your name?" I ask her.

"Maria."

But as soon as she saw me take the pencil to note her
name, she perked up, stretched out her shriveled hand,
and stopped me.

"Marigitsa!" she said, with barely perceptible emotion.

It was as though she wanted, since her name would
be perpetuated in writing, to rescue her second, affectionate name, that which awakened in her memory the
sweetest moments of her life.

"Marigitsa," she repeated as if afraid I hadn't heard.
"Marigitsa . . ."

I delighted to see, even in woman's most dilapidated body, femininity taking such deep root.

"And what's all this here?" I ask her.

"Eh, can't you see, my child? Rocks!"

"Then why do people come to see them?"

The old woman hesitated for an instant. Then, lowering her voice, she asked me:

"Are you a foreigner?"

"No, Greek."

She became more confident, shrugged her shoulders.

"Simple-minded Franks!" [1] she said, bursting into laughter.

It was not the first time that I'd seen the old women who watch ancient temples or churches laugh, disbelieving, at the holy relics they guard. They had long since become acquainted, kept them company day and night, and were by now indifferent to them. They knew quite well that for as many years as they lived together, not even one miracle had been performed. And they looked on the naïve worshipers with a roguish, skeptical eye. An old woman in Crete who was guarding some columns in her husband's absence told me one day as she pointed out two foreigners who had come from the ends of the earth: "Till now, my boy, I admitted as there were seventy-seven kinds of madness. Now I see there're seventy-eight!"

Old Marigitsa watched happily as I ate the figs and nibbled at the tangy grapes that she had brought me.

"And what do you have to say," I asked, teasing her, "about politics?"

"Well, my child," she replied with unexpected pride, "well, my child, we here are far removed from good and evil."

We, that is, the temple and I; and she pronounced "removed" with the proud tone that meant "far above." I was delighted. Much more than the temple the phrase of the old woman filled my heart.

I roamed about among the columns. It had rained two days before and the water still lay unmoving and clear in the hollows. I bent over and saw fluffy white clouds deep in the water, fantasies with a thousand shapes, floating lightly, hurriedly by. I remembered how, in the Far East, they worship the deity in basins of water above which the clouds pass . . .

At that moment I heard footsteps and French voices and saw the old woman jump up happily in welcome. I emerged from the columns—they were the two Frenchwomen whom I had encountered at the fortress of Clermont; and behind them, bantering and jolly, their youthful companion. I was preparing once more to retreat down the mountain when I heard one girl shout to the youth:

"Mr. Mastorakis!"

I turned, surprised.

"Mastorakis?" I said, approaching the youth. "What sort of name is that?"

"I'm Cretan," the youth replied, laughing. "From Aghios Nikolaos of Mirabello."

"And you don't speak Greek?"

"Of course! 'Good morning, good evening, I love.' "

"Nothing else?"

"Nothing else."

He told me his father was Cretan, but that he himself had been reared in Paris by his French mother, and that this year, for the first time, he had gone to Crete, tried on *vrákes*[2] and had his picture taken, learned three words, eaten carob and citron and bought a turquoise necklace, like those worn by horses as amulets, and made a belt of it. He spoke playfully and with emotion, making sport of his emotion. The two girls, teachers in Paris, came up. The first skirmishes of conversation began, the first explorations to discover with whom you are speaking, what vocabulary you should use, and to what extent you can expose your thought.

The conversation caught fire in an instant; one of the girls had just come from Spain, she said a few words about the blood-soaked earth that we all loved, and all at once the temple, the serenity of the landscape and the ancient harmony disappeared. All the holy opium which we had been taking these last few days—perhaps in order to forget contemporary horror—lost its effect, and once again we clearly saw the agonies of the present.

"I could no longer endure the things I saw," the girl said. "I couldn't sleep, I knew I'd fall ill. So I've come here to Greece to roam about, enjoying myself as never before in my life, and to forget. All mankind should pass through the lofty sanatorium of Greece in order to be cured."

We became friends. As long as I was immersed in the past, every acquaintance was superfluous and undesirable. But now, when contemporary necessity suddenly leaped up before me, I felt my bond, and the sweetness of my bond, with men.

We strode conversing down the mountain; ancient Greece had been dispelled from my mind like a slight intoxication. We followed shaded trails amid oaks and plane trees, passed by a cemetery guarded on all sides by swordlike cypresses, and arrived in Andritsaina. A wild village, full of hills and rocks, with a fountain at its center surrounded by chairs, where they speak of Athens as a distant, prodigal Babylon, filled with ministries. Bazaar day today; old women are seated in a line on the stones selling white figs, onions, tiny dried beans and heaps of fragrant yellow melons.

We got into a car. It was afternoon by then; clouds had gathered and were coursing rapidly overhead, casting immense shadows high up on the mountains and below in the valley. The landscape smiled and frowned, showed a strange psychic turbulence, lost its serenity. And when we caught sight of the famous fortress of Karytaina high atop a hill, we sensed that today, in such uneasy light, amid such contemporary concerns, this fortress, savage, stark and warlike, expressed more faithfully than any Greek temple the landscape around and within us. At its feet flows the Alpheos, the Chelmos gleams at the depths of the horizon. Karytaina, with its narrow lanes and old houses, with its Byzantine churches and rugged soul, is truly the Toledo of Greece. The abandoned fortress, ash gray like a hawk, stands atop the summit keeping the vigil.

Ancient temples are the products of joy and triumph.

Before them came Dorian fortresses, pre-Hellenic Larissas, Cyclopean walls. Then came balance and serenity. I gaze at the fortress of Karytaina and sense the soul of true contemporary man erect there on high, keeping watch. Later, much later, new joy and harmony will again follow the victory. Today, when we rouse ourselves but little from the intoxication of ancient beauty, we grasp how faithfully and pitilessly this fortress expresses our fearful moment.

Let us accept it, not merely with resignation, but rather with proud dignity; it is the only instant that has been given us, and within this instant alone is it our destiny to be valiant or cowardly.

■ THE OLD MAN
OF THE MOREA

■ IN THE EARTH and marshes along the banks of the Elisson, cutting a path through the willows and reeds, we search for the remains of ancient Megalopolis. It was built by Epamenondas to serve as a point of attack against Sparta. He girded it with three kilometers of strong walls and towers, according to the most exhaustive rules of fortification of that time. He built great temples, gymnasiums, arcades, markets, assemblies. Gathering souls from forty Arkadian cities he set them, either peacefully or by force, to populate his splendid new fortress. The Spartans flung themselves at it to demolish it, but were turned away defeated; the huge theater, Greece's largest, which could accommodate 20,000 spectators, frequently resounded with the victories of Megalopolis. And now we search among the weeds for Megalopolis and cannot find it. The Great City has become, just as Strabo remarked long ago, a Great Wasteland. Recent rains have flooded the theater; beneath the green water we could make out rows and steps, like seeing a submerged city at the bottom of the sea.

I cut a flowering willow branch and went down to the

station, trying to eject impromptu thoughts about futility from my mind. In order to be able to live and create, a man of action must limit his obligation to a narrow space of time. He must put blinders over his eyes, like a horse at the wheel well, narrow his visual horizon and devote himself to work. If his view encompasses great expanses of time, he is lost. He will see cities take shape and then dissolve like mist, and the works of man scattered like autumn leaves. He will perceive the fourth dimension; within an instant he will see the tree take seed, grow, blossom and bear fruit, and simultaneously rot away. A tree or a great empire.

Piles of melons and watermelons at the railway station; a peasant was emptying sacks of the heavenly fruit and cursing, distraught:

"They shout: 'Work, cultivate the earth!' Well, we work it, we grow thousands of melons, but who'll buy them? At a drachma an *oka*, who'll buy them? Where're the means of shipment? Take them to Tripolis—it's not worth the trouble! So the pigs eat them!"

Two youngsters came up to me, poetical pullets. It seems they had taken me for a scholarly type, so began to discuss art and poetry. Our country has been reduced to three most favored "schools"—Palamas, Karyotakis and Kavafis.[1] These two youths had the latter two deceased as their leaders; one, curly-headed and more vigorous, espoused Karyotakis; his intense youth surely had brought him the melancholy of overabundant strength. The other, stout, fleshy and lazy, declared the venerable Alexandrian Narcissus his chief.

For some time they wallowed about in these bogs; I listened, but couldn't participate and answer their questions—because I had plunged my mouth with hunger into a watermelon.

Finally the train came and I escaped. There is nothing more futile and tedious than aesthetic theory. Art is technique, poetry is a ceaseless working of language, of verse, of rhythm. It is a demanding daily act, without romantic exaltation. When you are twenty years old and living in the provinces, when you want to banish boredom and react to the householders round about you, the aimless linguistic controversies take on purpose, lighten the blood, exercise tongue and mind. But when you finally mature, have done with words and throw yourself into the sensuous daily ordeal of work, and then hear art being discussed, you slice open a watermelon and plunge in.

Next day, as I wandered through Tripolis, I felt unexpected excitement. Man's body is unburdened in the clean, lofty air. The stores, the bazaars, the greenery, the narrow lanes all recall a Turkish city—you are startled not to see latticework, minarets, and Negro eunuchs, and *hanums* going slowly by, faces shining tenderly from behind their filmy veils. Romantic predilection suddenly grips you—jasmine, *santouri, amanés*, fountains, and the laughter of women from behind high, forbidding walls. The harem of Hursit, which fell into Greek hands and was savored by the fiery fustanella wearers; and then returned to old Hursit who ordered all of his women sewn in sacks and thrown into the sea. . . . Sensuousness and cruelty, love and death, jasmine and blood—all the sweet-tasting poison of the shadowy Orient.

The chemical interaction of an external stimulation in the heart is a strange thing. From this Turkish city with the refreshing air sprang all these lascivious associations. Walking rapidly to escape, I reach the great square, in the midst of the populace. The entire Greek paradise; chairs in abundance, newspapers, coffee, water, peanut vendors.

Nowhere have I seen such alert, vital, cunning physiognomies. I prick up my ears to catch the conversation. Two shepherds stand in the middle of the square, leaning on their staves. One asks:

"When they catch a thief two hours after the robbery, is it considered 'in the act'?"

The other sheepman bends over, scratches his head, considering.

"What did he steal?" he asks.

"I'm not telling you that! It's my own affair. I'm asking you if it's in the act."

"If they nab him with the stolen goods in his hands?"

"But, poor fellow, 'in the act' means: 'I catch you while you're doing it'—understand?"

"But that's what I'm saying myself. If they catch him while he's with—"

The quarrel burst out.

"Not with the goods—*in* the goods! Understand? There's a difference!"

Suddenly they notice me eavesdropping, lower their voices and move further on, continuing with passion;

now they're holding their staves like pens and writing on the air.

I took a seat in a *kafeneion*. The coffee and water came. Today is Sunday, services are over, and now the householders proceed to the square. Dressed in their Sunday best, grim and pompous. They sit down, light their cigarettes, sip water and wait with faces turned toward the north. What are they waiting for? The newspapers from Athens.

React to the order around you, resist the current, say no! when all those around you are murmuring yes; this is one of the most demanding obligations of a soul that lives in a bankrupt era. Consonance and balance are fertile virtues in creative times; but when the historical moment of dissolution is at hand, a great struggle is needed to keep your soul in order. In order to catch hold, not to be swept away, a good method is to concentrate your mind on a great soul, one which sprang up and blossomed in your native soil.

Today as I sit in the Tripolitan coffeehouses watching the people and listening to their talk, I sense that if I were a young man living in Tripolis, I would concentrate—in order to save myself—upon the rich, aggressive, cunning and valiant soul of Kolokotronis. Here in Tripolis, air and mountains are still filled with his ample breath. From the days he spent as a merchant in Zakynthos, gazing at the mountains of the Morea across the way, sighing:

> *I see the spreading sea, and afar the Morea,*
> *Grief has seized me, and great yearning . . .*

until his censure by the land that he liberated, and those final serene moments when Charon found him, Kolokotronis' life was a dramatic, characteristic unfolding of a rich modern Greek soul: faith, optimism, tenacity, valor, a certain, practical mind, deceptive versatility, like Odysseus.

When the penpushers all lost their bearings, or the tin-soldier generals bickered among themselves, Kolokotronis would see the simplest, most effective solution. Gentle and softhearted when it served the great purpose, harsh and savage when necessary. Harsh and savage most of all with himself. When he served as a corsair on the "black ships" he once found himself without tobacco. He opened his pipe and scraped it in order to get some burned tobacco to make a cigarette. But at the same instant that he started to smoke, he felt ashamed. "Here's a man for you," he muttered to himself with scorn. "Here's a man who wants to save his country, and can't even save himself from an inconsequential habit." And he flung the cigarette away.

Thus he conditioned and hardened himself, in order to be prepared. For years in foreign armies he studied the art of war, the "manual of arms"; aboard ship he learned the *risalto*, the assault; he made himself ready. And when the revolution burst out he was primed, fifty years old by then, organized from top to toe. Armed to the teeth. He had amassed knowledge by the quintal, cunning, bravery, wide experience; he wrought songs to relieve his "yearning"; by contributing an axiom at a crucial moment he would silence the unorganized chatter. Our modern Greek problems have not yet found more profound, humorous and epigrammatic expression.

Following the liberation, when all the schoolmasters descended upon artless, tiny Greece, wanted her to be dressed in archaic fashion, speak ancient Greek, and be governed in ancient ways, Kolokotronis shook his sage, sober head with scorn and anger.

"My king, you've made a mess of Greece!" he told Otto. "For the first ten years you should make it fifteen Turkish and five Frankish, after ten more years, ten Turk and ten Frank; after another ten years five Turk and fifteen Frank, and finally, after another ten years, all Frank."

Unwavering mind, penetrating judgment, steel; with his eagle's eye he saw the great laws that are so confused and entangled by logical analysis as they really are: simple and omnipotent; woe to him who leaves the path to follow his own rebellious route.

He saw simply, and thus clearly. Once, at the welcome of Otto, a schoolmaster—who believed that by bringing back the ancient word he brought back ancient Greece shouted to the *pallikaria* drawn up for the royal salute: "*Pyr krotovole!*" He shouted, shouted again; nothing. The warriors couldn't understand. Then Kolokotronis leaped up: "Fire, my lads!" he roared, and immediately the joyous reports resounded.

Thus the Old Man of the Morea visualized and solved all difficulties, simply and directly. Without being led astray by either the "ancients" or the "Franks."

Nor by the local despots, nor by the Turks. In his most trying, bitterest moments his mind held fast its balance, not losing its freshness. When they sent a unit of soldiers to seize him in the little house near Nafplio where he spent his last days, the Old Man calmly opened the door. "What's the need for such an army," he said, "to take me to prison? It would have been enough to send me a furry dog, of the sort that runs errands, with a letter and lantern at his throat."

He had both impulse and restraint, he knew how to retreat so that he could advance; hemmed in by enemies, Greeks and Turks, he was forced to mobilize all his bravery and wile so that the Race would not be lost. Often all would desert him, he would be left alone in the mountains, and then burst out weeping. He sobbed like the Homeric heroes, with his long hair and helmet; he sobbed and was refreshed. He regained his fortitude, formulated new schemes in his mind, sent off messages, involved the elders once more, mocked the Turks, conciliated the Greeks; and the struggle began again.

"A rustic who hasn't got a shred of property in our lands has come to sit on our heads!" said the great names, the wealthy lords of the Morea.

But they didn't realize that this rustic, this pauper, had within him a creative whirlwind that caught up all the raw material—reaction, laziness, malice—and forced it to revolve around him, to take the shape that he wished, to become free Greece.

Kolokotronis, with all his faults and virtues, is one of the leaders of our race. Here in Tripolis, which he took with mind and sword, his scent still lingers dissipated in the air; with patience and concentration a youth should be able to reconstruct, as model and guide, the peerless Old Man. And thus, with a struggle now invisible and spiritual, to reconquer and ravish Tripolis.

I get into the car, in a hurry to come face to face with Sparta. I remember well, from other journeys, the flowering plain, the ancient grass-choked marble, and beyond, Mistra, with its fascinating churches and ruined palaces, with the heavy crown of its fortress. I've beheld this spectacle many times, but I know that man never twice crosses the same river; the world is renewed, and I shall see a new Sparta. The world is not renewed, man is, and the river that we cannot cross twice is that river within us. For this reason I'm hurrying to see, confronting Sparta, if my soul has been renewed.

Once, in the spring, I had visited Mistra with a woman. The lemon trees were in bloom; so intoxicating was their perfume that the woman leaned against a rock, almost fainting.

Another time, along with Sikelianos, I had paused outside of Sparta. A curious flower upon a fence had caught our eye, we stopped to pluck it. Children clustered around us.

"What do you call this flower?" we asked.

No one knew. Then a dark-haired little boy jumped up:

"Auntie Lenio will know!" he said.

"Run and call her!" we told him.

The little boy ran off toward the town, and we waited, holding the flower. We admired it, sniffed it, but were impatient, we longed for the word. And then, in a short while, the boy returned.

"Auntie Lenio," he said, "died day before yesterday."

Our hearts constricted. We sensed that a word had perished; perished, and now no one could place it in a verse and render it immortal. We were terrified. Never had death seemed to us so irrevocable. And we left the flower spread out on the fence, like a corpse.

Woman, friendship and art filled my heart then. I envisioned a Sparta redolent with the aroma of Helen, or filled with the rugged youths who flogged their bodies around the temple of Artemis Orthia, to fashion them into an impregnable wall for their race. What Sparta awaits me now? In its face I shall clearly see my own, present face.

We pass vineyards, mulberry trees, cypresses. In the car, the square-shouldered driver, who must have just returned from America, is talking with the peasant seated beside him.

"Over there they know how to live!" says the driver haughtily. "Not here! There, you should know, everyone is an altruist."

But the peasant can't understand.

"What's an altruist?" he asks.

"A man who sacrifices his last dime for his own pleasure. For instance, every American worker has his own automobile—got it? Altruist!"

We enter a deep gorge, reach Kokkini Loutsa, pass the inn of Vourlia. Before us, Lakonia, rich earth, slender cypresses; and in the distance, full-armed, uncompromising, erect, the cruel lawgiver of Sparta, the precipice-filled Taygetos. The captivating, fertile valley spreads out at its feet like a woman. The landscape is all sweetness and bravery, the soul is stimulated to great works, and at the same instant, like a flowering lemon tree, the breath of Helen clouds our mind. Involuntarily, gazing high up at the Taygetos, you murmur the heavenly verses of the great poet:[2]

From the peaks of Taygetos with ice forever
gleaming silver
in the lightning flash of spring, in the gold-downed
years of youth,
in a restless breeze soft blowing from the melting
snows
astride white steeds the matchless pair, the Dioscouri, descends
and bent low between her brothers who tiptoe
down the crag
in an immortal veil enveloped, Helen, like water,
downward flows.

◼ THE ENCHANTMENT
OF SPARTA

◼ Is THIS VALLEY of Sparta really so tender
and voluptuous, do its rhododendrons and lemon groves
really smell so headily, or perhaps does all this enchantment spring from the much kissed, much wandered
body of Helen? The Eurotas certainly would not have
its present seductive appeal had it not mingled—as
Helen's tributary—with deathless myth; lands, seas, and
rivers become one with great beloved names, and in-
separable at last, flow into our hearts. Wherever the
creation of a great poet's craving has passed—Helen,
Prometheus, Desdemona—there the shore blooms forever, the rock cries out forever, and the willow forever
droops and is stifled in the river.

You walk these humble banks of the Eurotas and
sense your hands, your hair, your thoughts becoming
entangled in the fragrance of an imaginary woman, yet
one much more real, much more tangible than the
woman you love and touch. And you catch yourself, no
matter how harsh and despairing that self may be,
whispering her ancient, caressing endearments: Andro-
fonos, Antheia, Afria, Doritis, Efippos, Epitragea, Thal-

amon, Makhanitis, Mykhia, Parakyptousa, Peitho, Praxis, Psythyros . . .

It was dusk. I strolled along the shore of the Eurotas; I was tired and content. I didn't want to lift up my eyes and confront the Taygetos because I know that all the serenity would vanish, terror-stricken, and my heart would harden. I would have wished to spend this first evening with Helen's distant, deathless fragrance. I had not come for her alone, but it is man's duty always to forget for an instant his most pressing task with Helen. And perhaps this moment of unfaithfulness—who knows—is the only certain prize of this earth.

Never has flesh been firmer, sweeter, than this shadow created by Homer. And never was flesh so fertile. When two Greeks, as tradition relates, went to greet the sage born on the Ganges and to ask his advice for their anarchy-ridden homeland, the austere ascetics of Buddha received them with jeers.

"These are the Greeks, eternal children of fantasy, the carefree fish that leap and sport in the fisherman's nets, and imagine that they leap and sport freely in the boundless sea.

"Their history is a dream, made from blue sea, from meager fields, ships and horses. They play and work with these elements, creating wars, gods, laws and ideas in their sleep.

"Unfortunates! For years you battled at Troy for Helen, never realizing that you did battle only for Helen's shade.

"You fitted out ships and set out all together, with

your leaders, prophets, horses. In your sleep you sailed on. From afar you spied a fortress, your blood caught fire, you cried: 'This is Troy!' Shading your eyes from the sun, you made out the black forms moving around the stronghold and cried: 'These are our enemies!' Your shadows clashed above the soil, broke apart and joined again for ten years!

"And all this, unfortunates, was but a trick of light and shadow. Helen, for whose favor you spilled your blood, lived unseen and untouched, far away in a temple of the Nile. For her image alone you besieged Troy.

"Up on the wind sat Mara, and created fortresses, and ships, and sea and the anger of Achilles, and your hearts demanding revenge and plunder, or, as you clamored: freedom or vengeance."

I imagine then that the first Greek would have thus replied:

"Even if Helen was but a shadow, blessed be her shadow. Because in battling for that shadow we stretched our minds, strengthened our bodies, and returned to our homeland, our spirits filled with boldness and adventure, our boats laden with copper jugs, brocaded fabrics, and Oriental women.

"For ten years we staggered on the shore, giving our blood that Helen's shadow might drink, gather strength and return from Egypt, and clothe the shadow once more with divine, warm human flesh.

"And after ten years of pleading and agony, she came. She came! When Menelaos lifted her high in his arms and, striding through the smoldering palace, the carcass of Priam, the thresholds of Troy and the pebbles of the shore, plunged waist deep into the sea and placed her aboard his ship, all the Greeks turned pale as they beheld the incomparable woman's beauty. The ten years flashed through their souls like an instant, and all the mountain peaks of Greece reverberated, as if touched by the sun, proclaiming the great tidings.

"Generations passed, but Helen still stirs in song, sits at the archons' tables and at the gatherings of the common folk. In the evening she goes to the beds of newlyweds, like a bride, and all the daughters of Greece bear her resemblance. She is the woman of the Greeks."

And then I imagine that the second Greek would step forward and say:

"Blessed be the gods! Before our blood and song gave her birth, Helen was a shadow, trembling like all women, without hope of eternity upon the earth. She walked through the canebrake of the Eurotas, sat at the loom, directed her servants, moved up and down the palace like a shade. She would have died as though she never lived.

"But suddenly the poet passed by and caught sight of her, and like the sea, the song rose up and took her.

"That's how we clothe shadows with flesh, that's how we combat and overcome futility.

"All the earth, ascetic, strikes me as a Helen, immersed in sobs and games, steaming, newly washed. She lifts her embroidered veils, and bending over with her palm to her mouth follows a man, the strongest; and as she raises her foot, her tiny sole gleams, bloodied like Victory's.

"All life, ascetic, is a shadow, and only the strong

man, with his labor and blood, can transform it to woman and make it bear fruit."

And the distraught Buddhist monk replied, smiling ironically:

"With your labors and your blood you've plunged deeper still into the snares of the Clever One. And the true Helen, learn it, learn it, is a shadow, a deceptive trick on the broad forehead of the Nonexistent.

"O futile dreams of a drunken, misguided head! How long will you be caught up in petty concerns, in insignificant pleasures; how long will you writhe like scorpions in the deadly erotic snares of earth, the Great Female Scorpion?

"Forward, arise, exorcise the nightmare of life, awaken and uproot desire, uproot your innards, shout out: 'No longer do I want!' Come. You shall become one with the soil, with the good rain, with the holy wind. You shall stretch out at the roots of the trees, you shall enter once more the earthen womb of the World, of the Mother. And you shall return to your homeland."

The first Greek, representative of all Greece, answered:

"I hear the world shouting. Around me I hear mountains, rivers, trees and animals calling to me: 'Give me a face so that I shall not be lost! Look at me so that I may live!'

"When I climb up a mountain and look at the marble, a murmur rises up from within it, as if gods and men were buried deep in its petrified entrails, stretching out their arms, crying for me to save them.

"You, ascetics, idly fold your hands and contemplate: 'Helen does not exist! Helen does not exist!' But deep within us, we Greeks sense that 'Helen' means: to do battle for Helen."

■ RUINS OF SPARTA

■ "What ancient said: 'The day will come when you will seek the traces of Sparta, and not find them'? In this cruel way the spirit is avenged. If you do not write a fine verse, if you do not sculpture a piece of marble, if you do not express an idea, any idea, with perfect form, suffice the form to be perfect, you are lost. Whether you are an individual or a people."

Thus spoke an elderly poet, who today was my companion as together we searched for the ruins of Sparta. Born in damp, leafy Normandy with its thick and melancholy fogs and laden apple trees, he had longed throughout his life for the light of Greece, for the airy shade of the olive tree. And today his gray pointed beard glistened, scented like a billy goat's with the aroma of Greek sage. His blue eyes gazed over the Eurotas, the plane trees, the dry parched earth, and rejoiced not to see the ruins of somber Sparta.

"Nothing! Nothing!" he shouted triumphantly. "Nothing is left. It serves her right!"

"Helen has remained."

"She's not theirs. She was a lovely woman, like all the others. She would have fallen to earth and rotted, just like the others. But the poet grasped her, set her to sea in his dactylic hexameter, and now she sails on immortal in the memory of the white race."

I did not speak. Old voices within me agreed with him, other newer ones rose up in my heart, hissing hostilely. I pushed aside the weeds, clambered onto a rock and shouted, obstinate:

"There, the temple of Artemis Orthia!"

Sparse, meaningless remains of an ancient temple; in front an amphitheater in which they would have sat to admire the ordeal of endurance, where naked bodies were scourged, competing—which body could endure the pain most valiantly—around the primitive, blood-spattered idol.

"All the handsome bodies of the youths," said the old poet as he gazed despondently at the uncarved stones, "perished and turned to soil. If they had carved out one youthful form in the rock, all the bodies that gleamed around this altar could have been saved."

I fell silent. I too had drunk of art's merciless, magical philter. Life, happiness, glory, the entire struggle of man flitted by above the earth like shades and vanished; only the seal of beauty remains upon matter, forever unmoving.

But today man's pain has proliferated. Injustice, anguish and irrationality exceed the limits of even the most unfeeling man's endurance. In these few recent years the axis of the earth has shifted. That of the earth, and of the human heart. And in the most sensitive, spiritual seismographs the concerns of men begin to be transposed. Each era cannot sense deeply any more than that which it most needs. It makes a selection of all the ideas and events of time past and chooses only that which it can feel, assimilate and transform into action.

My beauty-enamored poet companion is too late to change his heart; all his virtues, which before the war had been in the vanguard, have now been left far behind, old-fashioned, useless, obstacles in a life which has itself been changed. Soon the day will come—indeed, it has come—when we shall not sense the grace, the nobility, the gentility of beauty, the spell of peace. An iron century; Sparta, the Taygetos and the Olympian pediment where Lapithae and Centaurs clash will give us the highest, most fruitful joy. Because they will faithfully express the savagery, violence and voracity of our age.

We took the road back to Sparta. Evening mildness; the sun had begun to set, the olive trees dripped light, and a few gold-laden clouds sailed toward the west. To our right and left prickly pear and cactus. A young girl went by; proud black eyebrows, ample thighs, carrying a basket of grapes on her shoulder.

On a level space a gang of some ten boys were playing soccer. Fierce-looking, with narrow foreheads, curly black hair, short, thick, hairy legs.

"Not a bit of breeding," muttered the poet, "not a bit of grace. They're barbarians."

We stopped for a while and watched the coarse game—my friend with revulsion, and I attempting to place the grossness and give it meaning.

"Let's go," said the poet, "we've missed the sunset.

Take a look at that cloud, doesn't it resemble a swan? And look, its beak has turned deep red."

The youths' clumsy game hadn't given me a single pleasure.

Today's Greeks must love sport and the body through loathing for the spirit. For them the body is not sacred because it holds the spirit; it is admired as a reaction against the spirit. Socrates would never go fishing for souls in today's gymnasiums. But, from the opposite extreme, the old man's poetic talk turned my stomach. Youthful grossness, senile sentimentalities; and I remained alone, caught between the two enemy camps. I laughed and turned, spiteful, toward my aged companion:

"Beauty today," I said, "is an opiate which we take out of trepidation, to forget. To fabricate artificial paradises, so as not to see the harsh life around us, to avoid hearing the voice of contemporary obligation. Each era has its own distinct duty, and in accordance with it man's highest virtue is defined. Once, the great obligation of man was to create and comprehend beauty. In another age, sainthood was the supreme duty; the superior one was he who, scorning tangible earthly riches, set out for the great blue wasteland—the heavens.

"Today, the supreme duty is bravery. Be fully armed, decided, prepared. Scourge your body, not because you loathe it, but rather because you know that it is your great weapon and that you must have it inured for trying ordeals. We have entered a new Spartan period on earth—bravery, frugality, discipline, and stern confrontation of life are the great commandments of our epoch. Today the coward, the undisciplined, the delicate one, is lost—he who today comes to Sparta searching for statues and charming embellishments upon the stones. Lift up your head, look at the Taygetos. It is our Mount Sinai of the present. Upon its chest today's cruel Decalogue is inscribed: 'Strike, do not spare your life, do not spare the life of your enemy; you were not born to rejoice and to love, you were born to arms. One is your God—I, War!' "

We'd come into the wide avenues of Sparta, the *kafeneions* were filled, youths were playing *tavli*, young girls promenaded, the papers from Athens had arrived, faces shone. My friend laughed:

"Look," he told me, "at the people's faces. Look at the Spartan youths playing *tavli*. Not one has heard your fearful commandments from the Taygetos."

How could I reply? One of the greatest griefs of a Greek traveling in Greece is the absence of any organic correspondence between man and landscape. The Taygetos looms like a sword above their heads. I know of no other mountain range in the world whose meaning is so palpable. Look at the Taygetos and your chest expands, petty calculations vanish, you are ashamed of the tiny, meaningless life that you have led, you suddenly long to leap forward for a difficult and dangerous march. Gaze about you: coffeehouses, faces yellowed by malaria, youngsters playing *tavli*, taverns with their *amanés*, whose languor turns man's stomach.

I scanned the distant slopes of the Taygetos. In the

shadows of evening I tried to make out, above Parori, that blue precipice from which they would fling those new-born bodies that were useless. Kaiada. Such a precipice should be opened in man's heart, and upon the acropolis of every city. But our Christian upbringing, our medical-care philanthropies and teary charities, the craving to save the superfluous, have so far resisted such a Spartan choice. But how much longer? Even now the insane, the crippled and sick are sterilized. Races are being cleansed. They are preparing themselves. A dark but certain instinct pushes them on toward salvation. But not all. Only those who grasp the meaning of our epoch and are in time to make ready.

No place on earth today is as pertinent as this chasm, where once upon a time a race attempted to create a new type of man. Of all the purposes which we might give life, the Spartans chose the cruelest.

Man must become like a powerful animal, fashioned for the chase. Lean, unsleeping, tough, his power coiled like a spring, ready at any instant to leap. From the instant of conception—and before—until death, the merciless purpose kept sleepless watch over man. Not even for an instant did it permit tenderness or gentleness. Aphrodite was armed, sensual joy was a demanding labor. Love was the result of struggle and victory, the child a stone in the living walls of the fatherland. Youths hardened themselves, they sacrificed dogs to Enyalios, god of war, whose feet they had bound so that he might never leave Sparta. So that their hands might learn the habit, they fell upon the Helots and slew them. Dance, poetry, music—but only as much as was necessary for the needs of war. The individual does not exist. There is no individual joy, no freedom. Life is a savage hunt; go forth to hunt and in one stroke the world is split in two: the hunted and the hunters, into organisms that are killed, and organisms that kill.

Every once in a while, such cruel necessity rhythmically returns to the earth. Life, surely, is not only a hunt; it is joy, repose, sweetness, beauty, smiles and kindness. But at certain historic moments it is solely a hunt. We have begun one such huntlike instant. Certain races have sensed it and leaped erect. Certain men have sensed it, and cry out, like watchmen, "To arms!"

My old companion must have understood what I was contemplating as I looked up toward the Taygetos. Upset, he turned and said:

"And if ours is a warlike destiny, let us elevate the ordeal to a spiritual level. Let the barbaric horror, the cannibalism of men, the beastliness of war cease. For years I endured in the trenches, and my eyes, my hands and my dreams are still full of blood. Why must we descend again to the beast? Is there no other way to progress?"

"All vegetarians," I replied, "all pacifists, sages, theosophists and sentimentalists, lift up their arms and cry: 'Peace, peace!' But life follows its own dark laws, which seem below man's virtue. Tragic is war, tragic are life, love and the soul of man. We live in the midst of agony, sin and uncertainty. We toil to seize whatever we can of these bloody elements, and to make of them spirit.

"We see only a short distance before us. Our eyes cannot embrace many peoples, or many centuries, all at once. For this reason we always behold incoherence, futile efforts, fruitless wars. But if you rise above your era, your race, your habits, war will appear to you as the most tragic, yet the most direct road which the spirit can travel.

"War gives birth to frightful agonies, to enthusiasms and unexpected associations. Imagine the concentration of power in a race at the moment it gathers itself to leap forward! Imagine the instant of its leap—what enormous mobilization, discipline and outburst! How does it happen with plants and animals? Throughout the year they accumulate, they grasp for strength from the water, from the air, from the soil and the sun. Animals devour plants or other animals, gather up and hoard away their strength. And then, the crucial mating time arrives: The animal, in the merciless erotic instant, expends all his treasured strength for the species.

"War is an enormous erotic instant. No longer do two individuals mingle to bear a child. Two great armies meet. Amid blood and outcry one is driven onto the other. One is always the man, carrying the new sperm; the other is the woman who accepts, cowed and weeping, the victor's seed, and nurtures it with her blood.

"War is the lawful archon of our time. Let us courageously serve our term of duty."

Thus I spoke to the old poet, who slowly sipped his coffee, and sampled *loukoumi* for the first time. The *loukoumi* had become entangled in his teeth, he choked, his gray whiskers were covered with sugar.

"How does one eat *loukoumi?*" he asked, coughing. "I'm gagging."

"It's first dipped in water," I said, and looked on pitilessly, with unexpected malice, as the past generation choked on *loukoumi* beside me.

▮ MISTRA

▮ MISTRA, FILLED with black cypresses, sun-baked churches and imperceptible bluish presences, shone like an hagiograph in the morning light. From amid the plane trees, mulberries and willows of the Eurotas the eyes are drawn to it and cannot tear themselves away. This holy hill where modern Greece was born has all the manifest and occult charms to entice the most difficult and indomitable soul. At its feet are the walled lemon and orange orchards laden with still-green fruits, and water flowing, chuckling. Children are playing, women are drawing water, girls are seated beneath the fruit-laden lemon trees embroidering. Once more, life has caught on in this earth, it has sent down roots and struggles to rise, to climb the ancestral hill once more. It is the first, the green zone.

Then the dusty, treeless ascent begins, narrow lanes branch off, and the ruined, wretched hovels of the people appear; doors gape open, roofs are missing, wild grasses have overrun the walls. Only the churches, noble Byzantine damsels, still stand erect and charming, stationed amid the wreckage: Perivleptos, Evangelismos,

Mitropolis, Aghioi Theodoroi, Afendiko, Pantanassa. It is the second zone. Here and there a woman, pale and disheveled, like a phantasm, appears from a crudely roofed medieval hut; an old woman sits on an ancient threshold, spinning; a little girl leaps up wide-eyed and rushes to give you a bouquet of acacia blossoms.

Further up the hill the aristocratic city begins, with the despotic palace of the Katakouzenes and the Palaiologi, with that noble church the Aghia Sofia, with the rich, deserted mansions: balconies of stone, towers, huge vaulted halls, battlements. No longer does any living man reside here. Only a few lizards bask in the sun on the doorsteps, green and attractive with their long tails, like noblewomen.

And at the summit of the mount stands the half-ruined rocky crown, the renowned fortress of Villehardouin:

> A *strange mountain he discovered, cut off from the range*
> *on high above Lakedaimonia and about a mile beyond;*
> *there indeed he much preferred as the place to make his stronghold;*
> *he gave command, and high atop this mount they built a fortress,*
> *and Mezythra[1] he named it, and thus they call it even now;*
> *a brilliant fortress he'd created, and a mighty stronghold.*

As we passed through the orchards and began the ascent, a little girl was coming down, her white kerchief filled with the season's first wheat. She was blond, as if descended from an old Frankish kiss, and had a fluffy red bow atop her head.

"Where're you taking the wheat?" I asked her, so she'd stop a moment that I might look at her.

"To church."

"And why're you taking it to church?"

"So the priest can bless it."

"And, what then?" I said, to enjoy the little girl's reaction. "Will the blessing do any good?"

"No," replied the child unexpectedly.

"Any harm?"

"No."

"Well, what, then?"

And the little girl, serenely carrying on the ancient wisdom:

"Eh," she said, "it's the custom."

It's the custom. . . . I liked it, here at the threshold of Mistra, hearing so simply stated from the mouth of a child, the great secret that silently links one generation with the next, one Greece with the next. Continue the movement of your ancestors; what if you know that it has no practical value whatsoever; continue a festival, a dirge, a dance, thus holding time's thread unbroken —this gives continuity, nobility and roots to the race.

I turned to watch the little girl with the "first fruits of the land" descending toward the church, and I rejoiced as though I had seen a child holding a candle, running cautiously so that it would not be snuffed out, to pass it on to its child.

The broad courtyard of the Mitropolis. In the center the ancient marble sarcophagus with the joyous cupids and marbled grapes shines in the sun. What are the wily, archaic demons up to in this Christian court? It is as if Dionysos has sneaked into the transept and eavesdrops on the mournful, so familiar cries of God being killed.

A merry, loquacious old woman unlocked the door and opened the windows; a little light came in. We can barely discern the fine frescoes of the Second Coming, and the martyrdom of St. Demetrios. The colors glow dimly, the passage of time has obscured them, year by year they grow dimmer still. A few years ago I could easily make out the Preparation of the Throne, the angels running, terror-stricken, the throne in the middle, empty and savage, awaiting the fearsome monarch. This last flowering of Byzantine art is vanishing, obscured by whitewash and smoke. The elderly sacristan stands proudly at the center of the church and points out the double-headed eagle upon a plaque in the floor.

"Here," she said, "stood Konstantinos Palaiologos, when he was crowned emperor of Byzantium."

"Was it long ago?" I ask.

But the old woman, who by now had the Mitropolis, its saints and kings in her control, answered with authority, as if reading some gravestone:

"The sixth of January, fourteen forty-nine."

For an instant the pale, embittered countenance with

the martyr's crown glowed in the dimness; the purple sandals gleamed atop the white plaque; but the sacristan stirred, and the vision disappeared.

The old woman lit a candle and held it close to a series of frescoes.

"The Miracles of Christ in Galilee," she said, and crossed herself.

Refreshing, cheerful colors, Pompeian composition, idyllic air, an unexpected love of life. Fantasy and pathos, daring expression, freedom of movement. By then the immobile Byzantine forms had begun to move, the saints smiled, children played in the streets, trees and animals found a place in the life of man; here in one corner of the Peloponnesos, shortly before the fall of the City, the eternal Greek spirit had awakened.

We came out once more into the courtyard. The jolly cupids no longer seemed to us intruding, antichristian demons; born beneath the plane trees of the Eurotas, they felt at home, and mingled like brothers—a little jollier, a little more clever—with the Christian angels locked in the cool darkness of the church. For a long time these saints and angels had been sullen and tremulous. Yellowed cheeks, wild eyes, closed mouths. But little by little they've been mollified; the cheerful valley —the lemons, the tangerines, the rhododendrons—laid them siege and they surrendered. The queen of this place is not the Madonna; it is Helen.

"It's the Marmara, the Marmara fountain," said the old woman, who noticed me gazing so long at the sarcophagus. "It used to be down in the village."

"But why did they bring it here?" I asked. "It doesn't go with the church at all! For shame! Don't you see? Who are those naked, dancing children?"

"They're little angels themselves," said the good-hearted sacristan, as if wanting to protect them. "They're little angels, so don't be scandalized."

Once more we head upward, and once more children appear, giving us acacia and sprigs of basil. The sun falls vertically, the shadows have compressed, the narrow lanes shimmer. Loosen only slightly the stays of the mind and these lanes will fill with midday apparitions. Byzantine warriors with their shields, lean, savage monks, gentle, big-eyed women.

The monastery of Vrondochiou, where we arrived, was the richest and most famous of all Mistra. A center of spiritual life, it had a large library, and its church, the Afendiko, is a masterwork of architecture. Here the despots, the lords of the Morea, were entombed. Ruins of cells, kitchens and dining halls are still preserved, as well as bits of brilliant-toned frescoes. A few brush strokes from the robes and figures of the old kings have endured. Certain of these saintly heads are superb, full of life and movement and pride, like Homeric heroes.

Further up, in the Pantanassa the door was ajar, the courtyard shone, the cells were whitewashed, immaculate, their settees carefully spread by a woman's hand. Years ago I had stepped into one of these cells, and suddenly could not contain my tears. How calm and fragrant it had all seemed to me, so far beyond our satanic, complex life. It was as though I had suddenly been transported to paradise. A paradise like this earth, nearly unchanged, but cleaner and more peaceful. A reflection of the earth in calm, deep water.

Today, a youthful and ruddy nun was kneeling in the courtyard polishing the copperware, and the warm red metal's reflected glow gleamed on her cheeks. When she saw us, she leaped up, as though corsairs had entered the monastery; and as she hurried down the court to hide in her cell, I enjoyed the violent flutter of her robe and her long strides.

A few hours later down in the Perivleptos, I was to see the half-obscured frescoes of the Divine Liturgy. The angels, running with the chalice in their hands, take just such hurried strides.

An old nun was chanting psalms inside the church, leaning as though in a faint against a column. Clutching her rosary with its tiny cross, she shrieked and cried out to God in the despairing tone of a tormented bird. Her eyes had become shrouded, motionless, as if blind. She cried out, she pleaded, all alone among the brilliant frescoes with their exquisite bright-green hues. A woman praying in a shrill, penetrating voice and opening her embrace to the empty air always causes a man inexpressible sadness. She is like a widow returning at dusk, gripped by fear as night falls in the deserted fields. Whom can she tell of her suffering? Who will watch over her?

Widow at nightfall on the mountain,
who will take her in?

We sat down in the reception salon. A pale young nun with lowered eyes and two gold teeth brought us coffee, a sweet and cold water—the timeless tray of Greek hospitality. Then she showed us the embroidery done by the sisters with their slender fingers: cypress trees and monasteries embroidered in green and brown silk; tiny rosebuds on a black field gleaming like lighted candles; towels, tablecloths, kerchiefs, embroidered with all our demotic embellishments—swords, shepherd's crooks, birds, flower pots, partridges, bunches of grapes. Inexplicable sadness; I touched all this multicolored, labored embroidery and my fingers burned. The nuns, proud and smiling, seem to be showing you their dowries, but you know that there is no groom.

Quickly I left, mocking my heart, which was ready once more to break. Mistra's fourth level still remained, the fortress. Far off, the valley steamed in the sun, the Eurotas glinted among bone-white pebbles, the rocks crackled in the heat, mullein, sage and marjoram sprouted up among the rocks that I passed. The fortress gate open, the courtyards covered with weeds, I climb ruined staircases and reach the battlements. What joy to be strong, seized by a lofty grief and to climb a mountain, all alone! I think it one of the greatest of earthly delights. Two hawks soared up from the fortress, rising, falling, playing in circles.

I sat down on one of the stones of the fortress and looked down to the verdant plain, and behind me, high up toward the five-peaked mountain. The old Byzantine capital murmured at my feet. Further on, somewhere on the red earth, Sparta had once stood. All this soil is leavened with human blood. Sudden turmoil gripped my soul. From all of this human sewage system, what has been saved? Where did the laws and labors of Sparta lead? What did the Lakonian women with their short tunics achieve, they who chose the athlete and mingled with him of their own free will, having one thing only in mind: to bear a son superior to them? And the Old Rock of our folk tradition, the precipice of Kaiada, where the cruel god of the race sits and selects —what immortality could it attain through its cruel choice? The adored generation, anointed with athletic oil, has vanished, just like a mob of useless cripples.

Then I heard a voice within me reply:

"Listen: Sparta, once upon a time, arose from these fields; from the banks of the Eurotas, rife now with fever and degradation, a voice soars up. A command. Joy to the heart that hears it. This command has endured forever."

"What command? I know; let us, like that people, be courageous; let us live and die like men, like the sorrowing last emperor of Byzantium setting out from this ruined palace before me to rescue the remains of the City, and to perish valiantly. And then? I scorn and pour out this wine drunk by the condemned to silence their trembling knees. Leave me sober to climb the great staircase of horror."

"Can you never cast off from you your miserable, earthen existence? Destroy it! Set Someone free within you!"

"And if I concede that these countless lives, by concentrating their joys and sorrows and their struggles, could create an eternal fruit, what value has it? And if I cut this fruit and make of it my own flesh, thought and action, what meaning does it have? Helen, the athlete, the emperor, who gave of their tears and their blood so that the fruit might ripen, will never know that their struggle was not in vain. So, what am I struggling for?"

"And what significance does the individual have," replied a scornful voice within me, "what significance does the individual have to be worthy of rejoicing? Perhaps you imagine that this entire onslaught was his? Perhaps you believe it was an individual who coupled erotically on the battlements, who gave battle for Helen, who valiantly shoved the bodies forward to be destroyed on the walls of the City?

"A wind, a song flits through the human reeds. The canebrake of man comes to life. It is not true that the sweetest flute is fashioned from the bone of an eagle; the body of man is a sweeter flute still. You too are singing, toiling to enrich the eternal wind with new melodies. The canebrake of the Eurotas withers away, but the song ascends, austere, obedient, deathless."

Thus, within an ephemeral, rebellious individual there sounded, one high noon, the fearsome Spartan call of the Race.

■ THE PROPHET
OF MODERN GREECE

■ Noon HAD passed, I suddenly realized that "my brother the donkey," my body, was hungry. I went slowly down, with my eyes fixed on the peaceful vision of the cultivated valley.

Very few places on earth have such irrepressible charm. It is not only the sweetness, the fertility, the femininity of the valley of Sparta; not only the fearsome, haughty mountain above it; but this blissful landscape with its harmonized contradictions brought forth its loftiest blooms—Helen, daughter of the Swan, and Sparta, daughter of the Taygetos. It has fulfilled its obligation. And now you sense it enjoying sun and rain and the unintelligible din of men with conscience at rest.

The body of the Virgin in the Assumption in Byzantine icons often reclines in this way, wrapped in deep-violet veils. Hands folded, quiet, weary, satisfied. As did the landscape, so the hallowed body performed its duty: it bore a son superior to it.

I went on down the hill of Mistra; as I entered the deserted lanes it seemed to me that I was one of those sunburned shepherds that sometimes appear among the strange rocks of an hagiograph, resembling the rocks themselves, running to see some amazing spectacle.

Suddenly, as I passed the half-ruined Afendiko, I started. Among the stones wandered a shade, thin-haired, staff in hand. I stopped, ashamed; I recognized him at once—Giorgios Gemistos, Plethon. I had been wandering about his beloved city since daybreak and not so much as a hint had crossed my mind. For years this last sacred sacrificial lamb, this pale countenance, this wearied and courageous hand had fascinated my heart.

"Such is my fate," he said, leaning against the top-pled pilaster of the church. "I'm of the generation of Cassandra; before all others I catch sight of the disaster and cry out, but no one listens. *Ah, toils, toils of a forsaken city!*"

"They heard you," said I, "when it was already too late. Better that way. If we were to pay attention to the prophets, all the ruin and rot would be repaired, left still standing upright in the middle of the road, obstructing life as it ascends. Why did you want to forestall doom?"

I waited for a reply. The shade quivered and opened and closed its mouth two or three times, as if wanting to cry out; but it no longer had the strength. Like a fish, opening and shutting its mouth, choking in air. And all at once, the earth opened and swallowed it.

My heart knotted; I knew that I had wronged the great visionary, the sage lawgiver of an imaginary city. He had not obstructed the catastrophe, he had given no indication that the quaking empire could keep its feet. What could he have done about the inhuman, uneducated, dissolute archons, so bereft of the virtues of nobility, who tyrannized the common people? What could he have done about those monks who claimed to forsake earthly things for the heavenly, and *create in themselves idle and sluggish habit?* He calls them superfluous, unclean louts. "He who is sterile and far removed from man is not saintly; saintly is he who lives and acts in the midst of society, and, as he perpetuates his species, becomes a creator of life and immortality." What could he have done with an army the likes of which defended the empire? Culled from all races, avaricious brigands and thieves, ready at any moment to surrender. He wanted nothing of the Christian religion as it had been reduced, somber, dogmatic, formalistic. Christ and Apollo united within him in a new synthesis, pure and bright, filled with Greek grace and wisdom.

This Greek loathed and despised the Orient. He condemned its turbid cravings and excesses; his desire was moderation. Quality, not quantity. "Become," he would say, "like the eagle, a kingly bird which has no need of the affectations and gilded decorations of the peacock, the symbol of the East."

Whatever organism lacks inner unity and harmony is condemned to death. The Byzantine Empire was reduced to a mosaic of ill-matched nationalities, which only force and fear could bind together. It has no inner cohesion, no unified soul, it shall perish. "Let us leave," Gemistos shouted to his soul, "let us leave, my soul, and carrying the Greek spark let us pitch camp elsewhere!

We do not wish to impede disaster; let the end come! We shall make a new beginning. Let us abandon the others to bewail the expiring City; we shall nurture a new Greece."

So Gemistos would have spoken to his soul; taking the thick scrolls of Platonic manuscripts he set sail and reached the ancient acropolis of all Greece, the Peloponnesos. And from its coast he went up to Mistra, the Peloponnesos' heart. Art and literature sought shelter in the despotic court of the Palaiologi, sages and artists came seeking asylum; darkness covered the rest of Greece, Mistra gleamed alone, resolute, upon the breast of the Taygetos. Frescoes unfolded free, refreshing, full of life in the churches of Mistra, and a new breath of spring began to play about the brows. As is so often observed in history, here, too, art and painting, first among the arts, led the way, proclaiming new times. Where the poet could not yet succeed, where the citizen did not yet dare, the painter took the risk and thus proclaimed, spreading such joyous color and lively movement, the advent of a new freedom.

At this critical, pregnant moment the Visionary came, and began to establish the new spiritual teachings through his words. Gemistos was a magistrate, a defender of the law; but the laws which he administered were inferior to his inner justice, so he opened a free school of his own to teach new laws. From all points they came, hastening to hear the new Plato; the great Bessarion from Trebizond, Manuel Chrysoloras from the City, Ermonymos Charitonymos, the renowned teacher of Erasmus, from Mistra. Up from the teachings of Plato the new Word sprang, impulsive and revolutionary, seeking to blaze new trails for man. Gemistos was no calm, Olympian philosopher, gazing at human passions from on high. Like all the heroes of the decline, he was charged with passion and impatience; he fought to make fast a youthful state here at Mistra in the Peloponnesos beneath the timeless light of Greece.

With anguish you read the memorandum he submitted to Theodoros Palaiologos, despot of the Peloponnesos: "Do not forget that it is not permitted to either individuals or to peoples to lose their last hope. Many whom the world has thought dead have been resurrected. When danger confronts us, hesitation cannot be allowed. Entrust me, if you agree, with this restorative task. I am anxious to undertake it, certain that no one else can be found who dares." With such faith and pride he shouldered the responsibility. But he had been born several centuries too soon—who could hear him? The Palaiologi quarreled, envied and killed among themselves, they summoned foreigners to kill Greeks. There was no hope. But the voice of the defiant, incurable visionary fulfilled its duty: It cried out, even if there were no ears to hear.

Gemistos' central idea was this: Tradition is worthy of respect, but living man is not obliged to obey it blindly. He must, above all, have Reason as his guide. Man's conceptions of divinity, of good and evil, of right and wrong, are not invariable; they change according to time and place; they are full of confusion and contradiction. They are not divine institutions, but rather human ones, that change along with man. We have an obligation, by examining the era in which we live, the moment that we experience, and the place in which we are situated, to enact those laws that must govern us. Prophecies and revelations are delusions; only man's philosophical reflection can disclose the truth. By pursuing it we shall be able to live and to act freely.

What is the great arena in which man can live and discharge the whole of his duty here on earth? Society. Do not live isolated, scorning life and its riches. That is sterile and inhuman. The Earth is beautiful, bestower of many delights, suffice it that man know how to enjoy it with virtue and moderation. The five senses of man are holy, because they serve the eternal essence within us. And of all the senses, the most precious is vision because it reveals to us the beauty and harmony of the world.

Today these commandments of Gemistos are common property of all men; in the era in which he proclaimed them, however, in the Byzantine years of sterility and decline, they were unheard of, and in the opinion of the monks, "satanic." "Idol worship!" cried his bitter rival, later Patriarch Scholarios, who slandered the "Hellene," calling him *sophist, more impudent than all those lawgivers of polytheism and swinish life born before divine order.*

But fearless Gemistos continued his struggle to fashion a new Greek world. Veneration of life, heroic temperament, love of freedom! This great harbinger of the modern Greek renaissance lifted up his staff to hurl down all cobwebbed idols.

He envisioned a new state, powerful and just, which would regulate and govern both nobles and people. His ideal regime is neither absolute Oriental monarchy, nor popular democracy. He does not consider men equal; each one has particular virtues and abilities, and in accordance with them he must locate himself in the social hierarchy. "We do not entrust," he says, "the work of horses to donkeys; but neither on the other hand do we burden brave horses with the work of donkeys. We use rather, in the first case, horses for war; in the second, donkeys for transport of goods." Gemistos' political ideal is monarchy interlaced with oligarchy. The "aristocrats" would be counselors. Aristocrats, but not, however, of wealth or ancestry; rather of virtue and knowledge.

Such a new state needs a new army, capable of defending it with enthusiasm and fidelity. A national army, not one composed of mercenaries. We must not trust in foreign mercenaries, prepared to betray us at any moment, to become wolves instead of watchdogs.

And most important: The Greek people is composed primarily of peasants. The enslavement of the peasant must cease. It must not be that he sows, and that sluggards—nobles, merchants and monks—reap the harvest. The land, he proclaims—also something unheard-of in his time—must belong only to those who till it, not to the nobility and to the church. He who tills the soil must become its owner.

Four and one half centuries before Gandhi he gave the great keynote to economic self-sufficiency. "Away," he cried, "with foreign textiles. It is both an embarrassment and a great detriment for a land which produces such abundant wool, flax and cotton to beg for textiles to be brought from the Atlantic instead of developing them itself and dressing in them. It will be an honor for us to clothe ourselves with our native textiles."

Thus Gemistos cried out in the wilderness. Who would listen to him? The laws of history had followed their unmerciful course, the Byzantine Empire had grown feeble, there was no salvation. The Palaiologi viewed Gemistos' proclamations as utopian, the agricultural question remained unsolved, the national army an unrealized dream, the monarchy unable to halt the law of destruction.

Gemistos died a centenarian, one year before the fall of the City. A few friends wept for him, with the accustomed Byzantine rhetoric: *The all-encompassing and all-holy mind, the most diaphanous and brilliant star of the firmament, he who was a god-filled bugle, a sweetly warbling nightingale, the hearthstone of great joys, lies dead.* But as long as he lived, they left him to cry out in the wilderness. Not only did no one entrust him with salvation, but he was ridiculed as well by the mighty while he lived; even when he died the persecution continued. His name was anathematized by the Church, his works were burned in a holy pyre. They did not even leave his body in peace to repose in his beloved soil. Malatesta, a Frank, took his bones and buried them far away from Greece, in the Church of St. Francis at Rimini.

But they could not silence his voice. The body was excommunicated, the bones were banished, but the voice remained, and continued shouting. And from the teacher it passed on to the pupils; the pupils dispersed through the West at the divine instant of the European Renaissance, spreading the word of the teacher. Platonic academies were founded; Plato, meaning freedom of the mind, strode across the lands of the West, and wherever he stepped, spring flourished. And so, at the very hour that the Orient died, crying: *Anathema upon those accepting Platonic ideas as truth,* the West welcomed the anathematized, and in another part of the earth the exiled Greek mind revitalized humanity.

Standing for a long time in front of the ruined monastery of Vrondochiou, so oft-frequented by the great martyr of new Hellenism, I attempted by recalling his struggle to placate his shade. My imagination made him tall, with wide forehead and long white beard, with large grieving eyes. Long before the others he had loved and desired. And they could not forgive him. His shade still wanders unconsoled here in the rubble of Mistra. His dream of a new Hellenism has not yet taken full shape. We are still torn between East and West. The dim Oriental cravings within us have not yet become light; we still bow down, spiritual serfs, to the West. When will the dream of the great leader of our race be realized? From all the contradictory, double-natured, rich inheritances within us, will a modern Greek culture emerge?

Until then the great shade will wander from threshold to threshold among the deserted buildings of Mistra. And a contemporary Greek who happens to climb up this far will always risk encountering him, ferocious and implacable.

▪ MORTALS AND
IMMORTALS

▪ HIGH UP in the enchanting church of the Perivleptos, hanging amid complex scaffolding in mid-air like a church chandelier, in his white smock, with palette and brush in hand, round-faced and ecstatic like the lions that gaze at you, manlike, from old Persian carpets, Kondoglou[1] appeared, welcoming me.

His eyes shine happily, because he knows that he is carrying out his duty; and his hands are charged with impatience and strength. He has suffered and struggled much in his life, but ephemeral things could not subdue him; how could they subdue a man who believes in God? When misery clutches him, he triumphantly begins to intone an hymn: *To thee, all conquering warrior, do I thy city . . . or: Let all mortal flesh keep silence . . .* The misery is thus exorcised, the earth itself is altered, and Kondoglou, with his rings and his checkered topcoat, with his curly hair and wide eyes, enters whole into Paradise.

It seemed to me today, as I stepped into the cool church of Perivleptos from the bright sunlight, that Kondoglou was already in the midst of Paradise. He

127

was surrounded by all the angels and archangels, the walls from top to bottom were richly and colorfully painted, like old, ragged, heavily embroidered silks. A nun with a trowel was calking the walls, and two young helpers, bent over and silent, scraped away at the plaster with religious attention, laboring to uncover the hands, the beard, the calm eyes of some saint beneath the whitewash.

Kondoglou takes me by the hand and guides me from scaffold to scaffold through his paradise.

"Look," he tells me, "look, look . . ."

A primitive little white donkey like a woooden toy, Christ astride it entering Jerusalem. The passersby are hurrying to spread out their cloaks for him to tread, children run up with palm fronds in their arms. Higher up, Christ is born, and the violet-shrouded Madonna reclines, crouching in the rock, which just accommodates her, looking in truth like some great root. Beside her, like a chrysalis, is the swaddled Christ, and above soar the three mounted Kings. I have never seen such intoxication. One lifts up his arm as if blinded by the great light, the others stretch theirs out impetuously, as if wanting to seize hold of a star.

Further along Christ is being baptized, fish of every kind swim about his body; two human figures are stretched out beneath, representing the river; just, they say, as a youth reclines on the Olympian pediment watching the frightening scene; the Alpheos.

Round about, high upon the walls, the Divine Liturgy bursts out. White-clad angels holding the ves-

"...savage in the light, with a metallic-blue glare, rises the Acrocorinthos..."

"...the redoubtable Fortress of Clermont gleamed...
square, wounded, but still erect." (Kyllini)

Temple of Apollo, Bassae

Temple of Apollo, Bassae

"Mistra…this holy hill where modern Greece was born…" The Aghia Sofia

"At the summit...stands the half-ruined rocky crown, the renowned fortress of Villehardouin." (Mistra)

Mistra: The Monastery of Vrondochiou

Mistra: The Church of Perivleptos

"Monemvasia—waves were breaking at my feet, and a huge, menacing mass, silent and without a light, appeared resting on the sea."

"The Great City has become a Great Wasteland."
(Megalopolis)

Monemvasia: The Church of the Elkomenos

Megalopolis: The Theater

"The abandoned fortress, ash-grey like a hawk..."
(Karytaina)

"The revered fortress shone high up in the dusk." (Argos)

Mycenae: The Lion Gate

Nikos Kazantzakis' grave, Heraklion, Crete

sels of Communion hasten with great strides toward the depth of the church.

Lower, two warriors with averted faces: nobility, grace and sadness. You see them setting out, curly-headed, with embittered eyes and compressed lips, full-armed for war. And they know that there is no hope. The game is lost. These warriors must have been painted a few years before the Fall, at the crucial instant of nobility and despair.

"Look," Kondoglou tells me, "look . . . There, the Sacrifice of Abraham. Take a look at this photograph, how it was before. You can make out neither the donkey nor the child, nor the knife which Abraham held to slaughter it, not even Abraham himself; only a bit of the face; no hand, no body. The salt, which lodges upon everything like a calcified layer, had consumed it all. Salt comes, layer by layer, from the walls, or is deposited by the mist. Nowhere else in the world have frescoes been obscured by so much salt. First of all because the materials which the old masters used contained salt: rocks, lime and the like. Then too, because the mist which comes down from the Taygetos is fearsome. Let the specialists from Europe come to uncover and revitalize the frescoes. They'll achieve nothing. Here the malady is severe, and the method which the Byzantines employed to make the frescoes is to blame. They used thick paint, with paste; so in many places the brush-strokes form a relief, and the salt adheres readily. Here we have no discoloration, as in many old Italian frescoes. This is because our churches are dark, and because

the Byzantines knew well the chemical secrets of paint
—thus their frescoes do not fade. But they're eaten away
by the salt lodging upon them. Look at the thickness! A
finger's depth!"

To and fro rushed Kondoglou in that Paradise which
he, with his restorations, was bringing back to light.
Heavenly forms were suffocating beneath the layers of
whitewash, and Kondoglou, it seemed, would suffocate
with them; unless he could save them he would have
no peace. It has been rightly said that every man has
under his responsibility one definite circle of things,
men and ideas, and if he cannot save this circle then
he himself cannot be saved. Kondoglou's is filled with
ruined frescoes.

"And they're not all," continued Kondoglou. "The
mist and the salt from the walls aren't enough; the
painters completed the catastrophe. Artists in the eigh-
teenth century came here to correct the frescoes, to
freshen them up. With the passage of time their alterations became one with the original paintings, and now
it is most difficult to distinguish the original from the
retouched. The original blue background was covered
with black; this is why the inscriptions have disappeared
—there are none in the Perivleptos. The retouching was
done with a paint and egg mixture, as on portable icons,
and covered afterward with a resin varnish; and now
all the alterations have blackened, because the varnish
turns black. Most of all the important faces, because
these, primarily, were retouched. And now we must uncover all these hidden miracles and bring them back

to life, but without touching or altering the original. Plenty of hard work; it needs patience, technique and love. If you don't believe in this work, if you don't believe in God, you can do nothing. You'll be overcome with haste, you'll be bored, you will injure the saints; you won't understand in what way Christ grasps the Gospel, nor in what manner the angel spreads open his wings."

I rejoiced at the lively definition of such a profound and disregarded truth. Whoever does not believe in God (or "in whatever else" as Solomos would have added) hurries, becomes dulled, lacks love and patience, and cannot understand.

"You're laughing," said Kondoglou, not divining my thoughts. "Does it seem strange to you? Pay attention to the method of work and you'll understand.

"First of all we scrape away the layer of salt that has lodged on the fresco. Sometimes there are whole lumps, like stalactites, and hard as marble. Enormous caution is needed to stop where you must, so as not to scrape the fresco itself. Caution, so that you'll see the few tiny marks left by the stitching, that is, the outline which the painter made on the wall so as not to lose track of the plan.

"After the scraping, the holes in the wall must be filled and the fallen plaster smoothed over. The uncovered fresco of course does not have its original brilliance; the colors have grown faint. But after certain operations the tones return and the painting comes to life. Those areas which are missing from the composition are covered with a neutral color, so that they won't irritate the eye, and the total can be thus grasped unobstructed.

"The areas that have faded are sketched out exactly above whatever remains of the old outline. Then all subsequent additions, made so arbitrarily by the retouchers, are removed, and we bring back the original. Then the paint is fixed—not, however, with resin varnish that would turn black again and bring disaster, but by other means—and this helps the frescoes endure the attacks of fog and retain their colorful brilliance."

Kondoglou looked around him with delight.

"That's how we've worked," he said, extending his arms, "and we've rescued all these!"

He spoke like a diver who has descended to the bottom of the sea and brought several drowning bodies back into the air. And the saints, the angels, the warriors and Apostles gazed thankfully at Kondoglou and smiled.

"See how they look at you!" I said to Kondoglou, laughing.

Kondoglou shook his head.

"They've not been saved yet, they've not been saved," he said, sighing. "Some things are still needed so that so much work doesn't go to waste. Will they be attended to? Who knows! In winter the churches must be kept warm with heaters, or charcoal braziers. The icons must be regularly dusted, coated with a special compound and polished so that the dust won't be able to settle. This is absolutely necessary for their salvation.

The frescoes were never dull; they were polished often in some way, perhaps with wax. A special service is needed to care for these priceless Byzantine treasures of ours. A staff is needed to work regularly winter and summer. The thick layers of salt must be scraped away in winter, because in summer they turn quite hard and are difficult to remove. The thin layers, on the other hand, must be scraped during the summer, for in winter they turn transparent and cannot be seen. Work on the paintings must start in the spring, so that we'll have many days of light ahead of us; when the mists fall, the church turns pitch-dark. How could we work?"

He fell silent for a moment. Then he took me by the arm and we went outside.

"Let's go and sit down for a while," he said, "by the Marmara. I'm expecting a priest."

We took the path and went down, leaping over the rocks. Beneath a large tree was his Anatolian wife, and his charming green-eyed daughter.

"Everything will be taken care of," he said cheerfully. "Everything. At first bats flew in through the broken windows and scratched the frescoes. Now they've put in windows and glass, doors have been installed. The bats don't go in and out any longer. We'll bring the frescoes of the Perivleptos to life, you'll see, and then we'll go and revitalize the paintings of the Mitropolis —that's where the miracles are! Tourists will come, Greeks and foreigners, and open their mouths wide with admiration. Why just recently an Italian cardinal was passing through. He looked and looked, couldn't see enough, he hadn't the heart to leave. 'This,' he told me later, 'this is true art!' "

At that moment Kondoglou's wife cried out happily: "Look, the priest!"

I lean over and see an incredible, ruddy-cheeked seventy-year-old Papaflessas[2] with his robes flung over his shoulder, climbing the stairs two by two.

"He's a rare type," Kondoglou tells me. "All strength, fantasy, freshness of mind and spiritual boldness. You'll like him. He's from Pontus, and he's named Father Panagiotis."

He arrived, threw down a bundle which he'd been carrying, stretched out his hand and greeted us. Then he started to talk. I've seen but three such old men in my life, men whose words, movements and eyes projected such dynamism. Zorba, the worker from Olympus; Barba-Andreas, a peasant from the village of Krasi in Crete; and Don Miguel Unamuno, the great Spaniard. And now this priest became the fourth.

He spoke of his years in Turkey, of his misfortunes and his joys. How he brought the pashas, the despots, the women, the Turks, gardens and minarets, the Aghia Sofia to full life before us! He leaped up, gesticulating, changing his voice and expression, becoming one with his hero—first a cruel and rakish pasha, then a serf, foxy and cowardly. In a difficult moment, when his life was endangered, he turned and told us:

"I could have given in and saved myself—but then what of the soul? What happens to the soul? It would've been lost. So Devil take the flesh!"

And again, in the midst of the conversation, he suddenly started intoning, to prove how sweetly and how correctly those from the Pontus could psalm. He turned to Kondoglou, grasped him by the arm and gave him pointers:

"If you want to psalm properly, Fotis my boy, at dawn, before you go to church, you must eat watermelon. You'll see, your voice will become *ding ding ding*, like silver. If you can't get watermelon, then milk and egg. But watermelon is better."

Then he turned to me:

"See him?" he said and pointed to Kondoglou. "He not only has a voice here"—he pointed to his throat—"but here as well." And he pointed to his head. "That is perfection! Some have a voice in their throat alone —what can be done for them? They're able enough, they're able, but they don't know how. And others have voices in the mind alone. They know, they know, the poor devils, but they can do nothing. Joy to those with voices in both throat and mind."

I listened to him, restraining with difficulty my emotion and delight. These are the living souls of Greece! You travel through cities and villages, speak with thousands of people, and your heart is choked with indignation and shame. Is this our race, these wingless bipeds? So this is how low our blood has sunk? Small merchants, dunces, schemers, enviers, petty thieves. And suddenly a soul leaps up before you which has reached the peak of the Greek mission—to unite boldness with knowledge, passion with the game. And then you draw a deep breath. Confidence comes back to your blood, and the profound conviction that this race does not easily perish.

The Greek race always has been, and still is, the race which possesses the great and dangerous prerogative of performing miracles. Just like the powerful, long-enduring races, the Greek race may reach the depth of the chasm, and exactly there, at the most critical instant, where the weaker are destroyed, it fashions the miracle. It mobilizes all of its qualities and in one stroke soars up, without intermediate pause, to the summit of salvation. This abrupt surge toward the heights, unexpected by logic, is called "miracle."

Our entire history is nothing more than a violent, perilous leap from destruction to salvation.

■ THIRTY-THREE YEARS
IN EARTH[1]

■ ALTHOUGH I TRIED, I couldn't leave Mistra without going up once more to the Pantanassa, to stand in a corner beneath its arching peristyle and revive within me a sorrowful, enchanting body, decayed after years in the soil. This Mistra air teems with shades, with mysterious voices, with the dead. A graveyard suspended in midair, beckoning above the hot stones, undulating like a blue-green mist above the olive trees.

At first I resisted; it seemed weakness to summon the dead one, but then after inner conflict I reached the certainty that it would be cowardice to thrust her shade away. I sensed that she thirsted blood, longed to clothe her throat with flesh so that once more she might speak, to fill the sockets of her eyes that again they could glimpse the valley of Sparta from the peristyle of the Pantanassa.

I took the very pathway that we had taken together, thousands of years ago it seemed, one Good Friday, going up from Sparta to Mistra.

We strolled along through the flowering lemon trees; their aroma was so intense that my companion stopped for an instant and swayed as if fainting. But she gathered herself together and went on. She glanced at me and smiled bitterly; her eyes were suddenly encircled by two blue rings. A green scarab which I had once given her shone on her white blouse. "Beneath," I said, "at its feet, a magic spell is engraved in hieroglyphics, and one night that spell will guide you to Hades." But that day at Mistra when she looked at me, so pallid, I suddenly regretted having given her such a macabre ornament.

To drive away my unease, I began to speak to her softly, hoarsely, of the agonies which tormented me then in my youth. I spoke with passion, as though of love, and I sensed the heavy air of desire growing ever thicker around us; stealthily my spiritual agony was transmuted to impetuous confession. As though two people were bidding farewell forever, one standing on the shore of life, and the other setting sail for death. They were hastening to say goodbye, as if it were too late.

We had reached the foot of the slope, amid the ruins. Unexpected sweetness and compassion had flooded her dark face. Again she turned to look at me.

"Salvation always comes when we least expect it, and whence we least expect it," she said. "Wait. I too am waiting."

I touched her hand as if wanting to thank her. Her hand began to quiver in my grasp, to give itself like a body. I felt the stern-faced merciless law descend again between man and woman. Ancient mysteries, Christian loves, the orgies of Astarte—the entire mystic identity of God and animal leaped up and came to life within my ephemeral palm as it led on the woman. How involuntarily, I thought, does Word become flesh in a woman's breast! As the spirit touches her, it takes root like a seed. For a woman the spirit is not a winged, immaterial power, as it can be for a man; for a woman it is the primal, wingless, plastic essence which contains all matter. It does not have wings, but roots.

At that instant the limpid, fervid voice of a child sounded behind us, singing with precocious passion, unknowing still, of woman:

> *The earth gnaws at my feet, the wind gnaws*
> *my hair,*
> *and a little dark-haired one is nibbling deep*
> *inside me!*

We held our breath. Suddenly the entire pathway seemed to sparkle, as though the rocks themselves had blossomed. We held our breath, following the voice as it moved away, to vanish among the trees.

"Ah, the song," I said softly. "The essence of creation, the voice of God!"

"And for me," murmured my companion, "pity for that child flooded over me, pity for myself, for all the world."

We spoke no further. We had reached the Pantanassa, climbed up and stood in the heavenly peristyle —before us, down below, the valley of Sparta, the Eurotas among the reeds and oleanders, and beyond, the untouchable citadel looming, the five-fingered one, the

Taygetos, standing guard over the sky. My companion leaned against a column; it seemed that as she gazed at the two-fold landscape she saw her own soul. For two days we had been enjoying the Perivleptos, the Mitropolis, the Afendiko, the Pantanassa. The paintings came to life within us, the dimmed colors lighted up, all the angels of the Divine Liturgy in the Perivleptos glimmered within us, freed from the humid darkness of the crumbling wall. And they penetrated to our very depths, with their stolid knees and folded wings, and strode through our souls holding high, with awe, the instruments of martyrdom.

And now, in the honey-green light of evening, how this same Pantanassa gleamed, like a Byzantine ivory chest, fashioned with patience and adoration to cover the fragrant breath of the Madonna! What unity, what integrity and grace pervaded it all, from the rough-hewn cornerstone of the foundation to the erotic curve of the dome! The entire enchanting church lived and breathed calmly, like a warm living organism in the springtime greenery. So much did all the stones, the ornaments, the frescoes and nuns and fragrance of the candles exist as organic components of the church, that it seemed as though all had been created at once, in the same creative outburst, one night!

"I never expected to find such sweetness, such simple, familiar human emotion in Byzantine paintings," began my companion. "Until now I've seen only harsh ascetic figures holding parchment with red letters and calling out to us to hate nature, to take to the desert, to die so that we may be saved. And I trembled to hear them. Earthly life seemed so priceless, holy and certain to me that I refused to obey their command; but I was weak, and shook as I refused, for fear of having violated some great commandment. When I would hear you speak with emotion and gratitude of those inhuman apostles of an uncertain hope, I was terrified; I didn't want to think of you along with them, I couldn't.

"But these colors, these gentle figures, Christ there close to the dome of the Pantanassa entering Jerusalem, innocent and smiling on the humble beast, behind him the Apostles with palm fronds and the people watching them with ecstatic eyes, like a cloud floating by and dissolving. And the copper-green angel whom we saw yesterday in the Afendiko, handsome as a youth, his curly hair bound with wide ribbons, with the impulsive stride and the round, steady knee! Like a swain, on his way . . .

"And where was it we saw that other angel, the saddened one holding his sword like a wing, as though returning from heaven because he found it vacant and so came back to walk the earth?

"With these paintings, for the first time in my life I can reconcile myself with the relentless Byzantine Pantocrator. The saints are human like me, the angels smile and sorrow like men, the kingdom of heaven is not beyond death; it is within my earthen and impatient heart."

She fell silent again and looked away once more toward the valley of Sparta. The sun had set, the sky turned red. I moved close and lightly touched her shoulder, as though I wished to call to her to abandon the plain, to return again close beside me.

"You are amazed at such joy," I said, "because you had never been able to discern the love within the stern figures and savage commandments of the ascetics. Now that the sullen mask has fallen and you clearly see man's eternal heart at last, you thrill because you recognize it. It is your own heart. Yes, you are the ascetic who sits beside the water caressing the lion; and with a palm branch you, that same self again, follow Christ, that is to say, your deepest secret, that which you yourself do not realize, leading to crucifixion. And the copper-green angel is truly your betrothed. That's why you were thrilled when you saw him. There, the meaning of the miracle of art. Beyond time and place, defeating details and reason, the artist tells of the life, the passions and the hopes of each of us. Only practice and love are needed for us to penetrate the symbols and begin to distinguish our own face."

The bells began, at that moment, to chime softly and sweetly for the Good Friday vigil. We moved into the warm canopy of the church. The Epitaphios in the center was covered with lemon blossoms. Around it stood the black-clad women, weary and silent, keeping the vigil over the dead. The nuns moved about quietly, lit a candle, poured oil into a lamp, and drew back. They cast more blossoms and April roses onto the Epitaphios and vanished once more. The whole church smelled of wax, like a hive. Other priestesses, the Melisses at the temple of Ephesian Artemis, came to mind. I recalled the temple of Apollo at Delphi, built of feathers and wax. . . .

Suddenly the dirge broke out, the women wept, and my companion's lips began to quiver. I took her and we went out, breathing as if we'd been saved from some great peril; the cheerful stars spread out above us, the air was fragrant with lemon blossoms.

"There, there," I said. "Calm yourself, don't be sad; tomorrow we'll pay a call on Helen."

By next day we had forgotten the evening's dirge and strolled swiftly, joyful, over the cobblestones of Sparta.

"Do you sense how happy we are?" I told my companion. "We, two humans, two tiny ephemeral creatures, two fleeting nests of a love as unflinching and rugged as the Taygetos, are going, after so many thousands of years, to find Helen." And so, with the morning sun, with Helen's smile diffused in air, our knees quaking with sweet, primeval emotion, we go together toward her abode. The world is choking in blood, passions are exploding in the hell of our contemporary world, but Helen endures deathless, unsullied and motionless in the breath of the superb verses, and time flows by before her.

I wanted to cry out, I was choking. All at once the certainty had flashed within me: this body is leaving, this woman is vanishing, farewell!

My companion stretched out her hand:

"The time has come for us to part," she said. "Farewell!"

And now I stand here all alone, in the peristyle of the Pantanassa, in the very same corner, counting, *and she's thirty-three years in earth* . . .

■ MONEMVASIA,
GIBRALTAR OF GREECE

■ WE REACHED Monemvasia at midnight; waves were breaking at my feet, and a huge, menacing mass, silent and without a light, appeared resting on the sea. The priest who had come with me in the dilapidated auto crossed himself.

"Aghia Sofia," he said, pointing out the rock. "At the peak of Monemvasia is the Aghia Sofia, great be her grace."

"And William Villehardouin?" I asked him. "William Villehardouin, that handsome and all-powerful prince who seized Monemvasia and made a Frankish church of the Aghia Sofia—what's to become of him, Father?"

"We ought to look to where we'll be sleeping," replied the priest. "Let's call Koliana."

We had come to a stop outside a combination dwelling-tavern-inn.

"Mrs. Koliana!" called the priest in a mellifluous Byzantine voice, raising his hands high as if in prayer and intoning: Hail Mary! "Mrs. Koliana!"

We waited. Above us the stars shone, the sea was fragrant, two owls hooted to one another from distant hollows with so much tenderness and grief that your heart melted away. Neither nightingale nor human ever invested a simple, single-syllabled cry with such passion. Perhaps because owls can neither warble nor speak, they concentrate the whole substance of their yearning, with nothing superfluous, into one syllable. And from that syllable hangs the life of the species; thus it has taken on such an irresistible, passionate content.

"Mrs. Koliana!" the priest cried again with the passion of an owl. "Mrs. Koliana!"

A window opened, a white nightcap appeared, beneath it a plump, innocent, round face, like a caricature of the full moon. The street was lit up as an obese arm, like an adolescent thigh, reached out with a lighted candle.

"Right away!" sounded a hospitable but sleepy voice. "Right away!"

The stairs creaked, the house shook, the doors opened and Mrs. Koliana, tall and pudgy in her nightgown, appeared on the threshold holding the candlestick; behind her were illuminated barrels, hanging fish and strings of onions. The priest was hungry; he opened his haversack, but his teeth were few; I caught a glimpse of him as I went up the stairs, rapidly rolling each bite and swallowing it like a seagull.

"Speedy recovery, Father!" I called to him. "You never did tell me, though, what became of dear William Villehardouin."

"Good night," the priest replied, with stuffed mouth. "Peaceful and unscandalized sleep!"

"I shouldn't like bedbugs, Mrs. Koliana!" I said entreatingly to the goodhearted woman as she made up my bed on two boards. "I shouldn't like any bedbugs. Is that possible?"

"It is," she said. "Guaranteed. And tomorrow I'll have some *barbouri* for you, one-half *oka* apiece."

I slept. Clean sheets, a pot of basil in the open window; below, the sea licked and nibbled gently at the shore. My blood assumed the eternal rhythm of the sea and wind, and when I awoke next morning, the physical repose gave me unspeakable pleasure.

I would have liked to see the renowned court of William Villehardouin at Andravida in my dreams last night, or later, the fortress of Mistra which he liked so well. He loved war, jousting and women, kept troubadours at his court, and had a retinue of eighty knights with gilt spurs. He delighted in welcoming friends from Champagne, the distant land of his forebears, and in loading them with gifts—horses, velvet cloaks and beautiful women. He was born in Kalamata, Greek was his mother tongue; he combined within him the caution and cunning of the Byzantine with the joy of life and audaciousness of the Frank. I knew what the books had to say about his life and wars, but all that remained unorganized within me, like the pebbles of a mosaic; only in a dream could they be whirled about and brought to life, could knowledge rise to its highest peak and become vision. But the night had passed quietly, unscandalized, and the dream did not come.

Day was breaking as I crossed the narrow strand, the

moni emvasis (single entrance) that joins the precipitous rock of Monemvasia with the mainland. I moved
on, gazing at the proud rock, not tiring of it. Until
now I thought that the finest thing I had seen in the
Morea was the fortress of Karytaina. But how much
more savage, imperious and isolated is this hulk of granite, this Gibraltar of Greece! At night it seemed to me
a terrible beast lying in wait; today in the light of dawn
it gleamed above the water like a monstrous anvil.
Proud men have always inhabited this rock. Wind, sea,
loneliness and poverty have hammered on their souls
day and night. They had no gardens in which to stroll,
saying: "Life is sweet, let us take refuge here." They
had no earth to till, to love, and to say: "This is fertile
soil, let us bow down, let's patch things up with the
tyrants, let's not lose it." They had nothing but the sea,
their merciless mistress. So they threw themselves upon
it, fishermen, merchants, corsairs. The Byzantine Empire feared them, and granted them privileges. They
lived independent, with their own rulers—the Mamon-
ádes, the Daimonoyiánnides, the Sofianí.

When the Franks came and subjugated all Greece,
here they came to a halt, gazing high up, and their
horses refused to go on. But William Villehardouin
turned obstinate: "I've nothing," he shouted, "I've
nothing if I don't have Monemvasia!" He called for aid
from the great lord of Athens, the three barons of Eu-
boea, the duke of Naxos, the count of Kefalonia, and
from faraway Venice. He encircled the wild rock by
both land and sea, bombarded it with stones from the

catapults, made assaults. He threatened, pleaded; nothing. For more than three years the Greeks held out. But at last their supplies were exhausted.

They did not have a bite to eat, only one another;
so they made their meals of rats, and of cats as well.

"We'll surrender the fortress," declared the despairing Monemvasiots, "but both we and our property shall remain independent and untaxed, free from any servitude; we shall work only our boats, and for a wage."

Villehardouin accepted. And then the three archons of Monemvasia, Mamonás, Daimonoyiánnis and Sofianós, silently crossed over the *moni emvasis*, reached the Frankish encampment and handed over the great iron keys to the fortress.

The prince, a prudent man, greeted all of them.

But he enjoyed it only a few years.

There is no end to the bliss that history's hashish can give the human heart when suddenly it is caught unguarded and remiss. Consider the history of man and you are drugged, as if hearing a tale of blood, love and mourning. But as I went through the covered gate of the city, three children leaped up from the corner and brought me back to the proper path—Alexandra, Foto, and Manolas. It was as if we were old friends, and since they had no school today, they awaited me at the curb of the fortress gate to play. Manolas gave me one of his two figs, and we divided up the pomegranate that Alexandra was carrying.

"It's from my Auntie Sofoulia's pomegranate orchard," she explained to me. "She died last month; took a chill, the poor thing. My father slaughtered a lamb, undressed her and wrapped her up in the warm skin. That's what they told us to do so she'd get well. But she suffocated."

Manolas burst into laughter.

"Wouldn't he have done better, say I, to give her quinine!" he said.

"If she were alive we wouldn't be eating pomegranates," said Foto with her mouth full. "You keep still!" she added angrily, glancing toward Manolas.

It looked as though there was a danger of Sofoulia taking the quinine prescribed by Manolas and being resurrected; and so not letting us cut pomegranates from her orchard.

The three children hurried ahead, eating and talking, and for an instant I stopped to enjoy the narrow ascending cobblestone lane that unwound before me. The first door on the right was a notary's office. A young man was seated at the desk in the back, and across the way, in a tiny *kafeneion*, sat an old man, speaking: debts, figures, lawsuits, trial expenses . . . I stood still for a moment. The old man was shouting, he couldn't bear the expenses any longer, he said, and he raised his emaciated hand in despair. Beside him sat a young village girl, his daughter or grandchild. Calm, assured, with big green eyes, and blue circles around those eyes.

She was smiling, gazing out at the street, paying no attention to either trials or relatives. Within her she felt a mysterious, indomitable strength. Surely this is what the Greek maids who tamed the Frankish brutes were like, who mingled with them, sweet and voluptuous, and in two or three generations undid them.

I rejoiced, as if with my own eyes I'd seen a great law sitting there in the poor *kafeneion*. I moved on. Old, low houses, cobblers, grocers, a barber shop . . . Two or three old men were seated on the doorsteps, a donkey laden with dry twigs went by. Tiny courtyards newly cleaned and whitewashed, cleanliness and the smell of burning wood. Red blossoms in the windows, basil, marjoram. A pale, slender girl appeared at a high window, looked out to sea and went inside once more. A canary hanging from a trellis next to a big bunch of grapes began to chirp.

Foto turned:

"Come on," she called to me. "Come see my father! There he is!"

And she pointed out a mason working atop a roof. One of his eyes was bandaged with a handkerchief.

"You know why he's got the kerchief?" she asked me, her eyes gleaming with the thought that I'd never guess. "You know? You don't know! Well then, I'll tell you: A few days ago our kitten put his eye out, and now he's working to get a glass one. Our kitten's called Blackie, little Blackie. . . ."

Tragic tales related with gusto; life on the rock is harsh, without sobs. The father lost his eye, the aunt suffocated in the lambskin, and the children accept all these horrible things like customary occurrences, well harmonized with this life of granite.

"Where's the church of the Elkomenos?" I asked my three little guides.

"Let's go! Let's go! Let's go!" they shouted, and ran off dancing ahead.

We reached a small square. On the right is an old mosque, now a *kafeneion*, to the left is the church of the Elkomenos. Foto dashed off, got the keys from the sacristan; we went in. Christ with a red mantle and bound hands . . . a fine Crucifixion, a Madonna with great, embittered eyes. Of all the icons, I liked most the Birth of Christ. Kneeling, the Madonna worships her child; all around there are rocks; shepherds descend wreathed with leaves and blossoms, sounding their horns. Further down, Joseph bends over in meditation; a shepherd watches him, leaning on his staff. Beside him, in gold brushstrokes, grows a bushy tree, and atop it a large redheaded bird.

"Let's go to St. Nikolas' now!" cried the guides. "It's got desks! It's the school!"

We took the upgrade. Fearful poverty; girls are winding thread, old women are spinning, the houses are clean and bare: a jug, a towel on the wall, a wash basin . . . Here and there a fig tree among the rocks. Yellowed children play quoits. Suddenly I stopped, delighted: On one of the sills was a large pot, made from the broken base of a lime-washed, banded urn. Each band was painted with the lightest pastel hues—azure,

rose and yellow ocher. I had never seen such nobility
of color. The humble vessel resembled a priceless porce-
lain there in the sun.

Inside the hut a girl sat weaving. Pale and depressed,
in no mood for singing, according to the demotic song:
Golden loom and ivory comb . . . But the loom was
of creaking wood, the comb was old, her grandmother's.

"What're you weaving?" I asked her, leaning against
the door jamb.

She didn't even turn.

"Dowry . . . dowry . . ." she murmured.

As if she knew that her labors would probably be in
vain.

"Come on, let's go! Leave Stella alone!" shouted the
three demons, and pulled me away from the door.

Again we located the key and opened the church.
Empty, only the desks and a platform at the rear.

"Look! Here's where we had our exams. I recited 'The
Orphan'!" said Alexandra.

"And I: 'How Can You Watch Us, Motionless?'"
said Manolas.

"Listen to mine!" shouted Foto and leaped onto the
stage.

I recall bits and pieces of the song she'd learned. It
went roughly: "I don't want riches, I don't want glory
. . . I want a heart that's pure . . ."

The little nippers had begun to wear me out. I went
outside and gave them something to go get candies and
decals and leave me alone. They stood with surly faces,
as if I'd spoiled the game.

"Just tell me which path to follow to reach the Goula, the upper fortress."

"Find it by yourself!" said Alexandra. "Imagine that!"

"Imagine that!" said Foto, sticking out her tongue.

But Manolas took pity on me:

"There, head right," he said. "Head right and you'll find the steps."

I took the path, saddened because my friendship with the children had ended so badly. To quarrel with one older than you often leaves a feeling of relief and pride; but quarrel with a child and a strange, ineffable sadness always remains, as if you have relinquished whatever freshness remained in your soul.

Shadowy arcades, labyrinthine medieval lanes, ruined churches; life again entwines among the ruins, deep-rooted like ivy—with crying babies, laundry, and the shrill cries of poverty.

When the Byzantines retook it from Villehardouin, the city reached its zenith; *prosperity,* according to a golden bull, *nobility of demeanor; and the practice of arts and crafts; and abundance of all things in its market place.*

I found the stone staircase and went up. On the right a wall for the protection of warriors ascending, a wrecked tower here and there. I entered the fortress through a gallery, came out into the central court, and climbed through the ruined Turkish houses to the large, impressive church of Aghia Sofia, built by Andronikos II. Wreckage, a few remains of paintings on the walls, an old Gospel on the altar. I opened it, to find a sentence and breathe freely. I opened at random, marked a sentence with my finger and read: "Caution, lest you burden your hearts with revelry, intoxication and the concerns of life." I shouted the great command again and again, and my heart was lightened.

When you find yourself in a lofty fortress, in the ruins of a great city, your heart may be suddenly overcome; not by great fright, but rather by a strange, defiant tenacity. As though the heart is a peculiar torrent which flows uphill, contrary to nature. Nowhere can a proud soul find more abundant nourishment than amid the wreckage of the world. Because there it clearly realizes that it has undertaken a hopeless struggle, and rejoices in the struggle because it awaits no reward. It struggles on this way simply because it is powerful, because it wants to play. Never, it swears, will I burden my heart with revelry, intoxication and the concerns of life. I shall preserve it always a flame, rising in empty air.

I sat amid the ruins and rejoiced to hear such a voice rising from the stones of Monemvasia. And for a long time I looked straight down, watching three goats with gleaming black hair climbing the red rock, directly above the sea.

■ MYCENAE

■ As I LEFT Monemvasia at daybreak it be-
gan to drizzle. The savage rock had turned a deep por-
phyry, and the sea around it white. All day long, through
a gossamer veil of fine rain we observed the face of
the Peloponnesos—its mountains, olive groves, vineyards, its villages and people, glistening, drenched and
shiny, all smiles. Just as we also see the face of the
weaver dimly gleaming behind the upright tracery of
the warp.

The Taygetos juts up from the earth, an unscalable
wall, and the female valley dripping at its feet laughs
and weeps in the fitful light. We pass through broad-
avenued, *kafeneion*-filled, widowed Sparta, bereft of its
gymnasium and its Leonides. There is a bazaar in the
square today: huge shiny tomatoes, onions, grapes, figs,
piles of wicker baskets and panniers. Briefly the sun
shone, Helen's garden at the museum twinkled—the
palms, the lemon trees, the roses. Outside the fence a
woman went by astride a white mule; just in time I
caught sight of her remarkable saddle blanket: light
green, embroidered with a border of little black cypresses.

We headed for Tripolis; in the turbid air the earth

has a strange, almost human tenderness; it penetrates more calmly, and deeper, into man's heart. Like a weeping woman. As if you are bidding the earth farewell, and your heart is shaken. Suddenly you reflect that the day will surely come that you must part.

We stopped for a while in Tripolis to eat. Once more the modern Greek faces, all cunning, suspicion and rapaciousness. How remarkably they resemble the Tripators in the Acropolis museum! The same pointed beards, thick lascivious lips and wily grins. Their little eyes throw off sparks, looking you over as if to say: "And just what do you think you're up to?" Here and there I caught a bit of conversation from the adjacent table: "So now the poor idiot happens to die?" said a youthful evzone with a black-dyed, twirled mustache. "Just when the trees are full of olives!" And another at a corner table, in a stiff collar, lemon-yellow and pretentious, with an officious tone: "Evolution, indeed, has made man miserable!"

Again I took the road due north. Women in white shawls are bent over gathering cotton. The fields seem covered with snow. Stacks of corn gleam yellow and red on the threshing floors. Here and there oleanders still in bloom, or a huge heliotrope with ripe, jet-black heart. We leave Arkadia behind; the valley of the Argolid stretches before us, serene and cheery; the sun has triumphed and driven away the clouds, the world smiles. We go through a village—doors are open, old women and children have come out with baskets to search for snails in the hedgerows.

And I am meditating on the last stop of this trip, the

fearful fortress of Mycenae, with the two lionesses—
Clytemnestra and Electra—erect at its gate. The gentle,
real and humble life of the village—the corn, cotton
and snails—vanishes, devoured by the ghastly legend.
How incredibly superlogical, or absurd, this life is—it
causes you to scorn reality for a fantasy, to be more
concerned with the house of Atreus than with your own
home.

"Begging your pardon," said the driver, one of the
most authentic of the Tripators that we mentioned,
"but what're so many foreigners up to there at Mycenae? And as far as the foreigners, all right, but what
about you? Begging your pardon, of course."

"But don't you know . . ." I tell him.

In a naive moment of weakness I found myself ready
to start "enlightening the masses." But the driver took
the wind out of my sails.

"I know all about it," he said with a grimace. "I
know all that stuff by heart, and upside down. Kastrou
hacked up Athanasopoulos who had just come back
from the war, the same way Clytemnestra cut Agamemnon to bits a few years back. . . . You can have it!"

"You've made a jumble of it, Yanni," I said, laughing.

"I've made no such jumble! It's just the same. Either
Athanasopoulos or Agamemnon."

"But it's not at all the same," I said, trying to find a
simple way to explain to him.

"And why, if you please, isn't it the same?"

"Look, because Aeschylus took a hand—"

"And just who was he?"

"Haven't you ever been to the theater to see an ancient tragedy?"

"Of course I have! What do you take me for? A complete blockhead? Once I went, but I didn't understand a thing. I only saw old-time burnooses and helmets like Kolokotronis', and heard shouting and commotion, what a fuss. Some sort of gods came down, fear and trembling. It began to thunder. 'There'll be a riot here,' I said. 'Get out, Yanni, don't let them nab you for a witness.' So I left."

We had reached Argos at last. The revered fortress shone high up in the dusk. Toward the left the sky was deep red; two clouds floated along through the blood.

"Do you know a clean hotel in Argos?" I asked to change the subject.

But the driver was irritated; he shook his head.

"And here I was expecting you to enlighten me!" said the wily fellow, as though disappointed.

But deep down inside he was deriding the simpleminded foreigners, and all other "learned" souls. I was ashamed, lest he make a fool of me.

"Then I'll tell you, Yanni," I said, to salvage the self-respect of the penman. "Did you know that a European once turned up at Mycenae, dug away and found treasure?"

"That's more like it!" shouted the driver, winking at me. "Tell me the story! So that's why I see 'em going up and down, clambering over the boulders and searching, their eyes peeled. That's right, now we've got it! They're after gold, that's what it is!"

The Tripator had solved the puzzle, he calmed down. "I know a good hotel," he said. "Relax!"

Argos. The city, the church, chairs, coffeehouses, glasses of water . . . Modern Greeks. Surly faces, sunken cheeks, insatiable eyes. They look you over as though you're a ram they want to buy. They search you with their eyes, examine your shoes, your clothing, your hat. They calculate. Uncertainty gnaws them— Who are you? What tobacco do you smoke? What have you come to their place to buy or sell?

Pigs wander through the streets, young provincial dandies sit in the *kafeneions*, but there is not a woman in sight. The entire square is filled with mustaches. A flock of well-fed priests. The church, ringed by *kafeneions*, shines gently with its yellow hue and lean, graceful belltower.

I retreat to the outskirts of the city, to the ancient theater. I climb the steps, the temptress sea shimmers, the rock of Nafplio stands, tall and threatening in the air. Further above the amphitheater is the little chapel of St. George, on the very spot where the temple of Aphrodite once stood. And still further, the Kriterion, where Danaus condemned his daughter Hypermnystra, because she alone of the fifty sisters refused to slay her husband. They had come, along with their father, as refugees from the land of the Nile; they taught the people of Argos to irrigate their fields and made the barren earth a garden. Poetry caught them up, they became Neraids, and so became immortal.

Along with the dusk, Greek legends descended, and the rows of the theater filled with shades. This soil suddenly became ennobled, and the dandies, the priests and the mustachioed men seated in the square shone. *Let us arise, and to Argos' folk now chant our prayer, for fair return of service fair* . . .

Thus reconciled, I took once more the road for the living city, sat down in the *kafeneion* in the shade of the church, and along with the modern Greeks ordered a coffee, two glasses of water, and four chairs. But the verses of Aeschylus seared my lips.

Next day at noon we set out for Mycenae. This is the vertical, flaming hour that suits these fearsome stones and legends. The morning light gives them a purity which they should not have, dusk gives them a romantic melancholy to which they do not condescend. Neither the skylarks of day nor evening's lovesick owls nest here amid the renowned, arid precipices; but rather savage, flesh-eating birds of prey, eagles and hawks, which balance at high noon on the peak of the wind, scanning the plain for quarry.

Strangling heat, the blood catches fire, the throat dries up. Excellent physical circumstances for this pilgrimage. We go up from Kharavati along the uphill track: I have my gaze fixed between the formidable peaks of Zara and Profiti-Elias, trying to make out the lair of the Atreids in the white-hot light. It is a rock among the other rocks, and you cannot distinguish it. But from the beating of your heart you sense that you are drawing continually nearer. We turned right, and the terrifying fortress gate with its two erect lionesses loomed before us.

"Here's the butcher's!" said the driver, coming to a stop.

I was glad to have with me the roughcut humor of the common folk, the tough-hided shield that romanticism and sentimentality cannot so readily penetrate. It weighs all on the scale of its firm and practical mind, which knows, and has long since admitted as legitimate, that life is rife with blood and perfidy, but then again, that we must not become too concerned; just as we are not terrified by a tale of dragons. "Life is a life sentence," we shall die and then see that everything was air; thus life itself is little more than a fable. Yanni the driver lived this timeless, rustic world view, and when he crossed the threshold of the Atreids, he felt his knees shaking not at all.

Just as we entered, the modern watchman jumped up from the left of the crypt hewn in the wall where the ancient doorkeeper resided. An appealing little old man with his cane, with his cigarette and with a gleam in his eye which revealed that he knew what treasures of legend, blood and stones he had been entrusted to guard.

"Is Mr. Athanasopoulos in?" the driver asked him soberly.

"Mr. Athanasopoulos?" replied the guard, his eyes opening wide. "I don't know him."

"Agamemnon, dad!" explained the driver, bursting into laughter.

The guard frowned; he didn't like them mocking the dead. Because then he himself would lose face; all the grandeur that was his in guarding fearsome things would evaporate.

"Pay attention where you are going," he said angrily, "and show some respect."

"The poor fellow!" said the driver, turning to me. "The poor fellow, the archaeologists have driven him mad."

Humor, gusto, rousing toasts and Thyestian banquets, Shakespearean quoits with human skulls. And so, as Yanni and I moved on, peering into the dragon's lair, I filled with trepidation, he with high spirits, I imagined a contemporary Aeschylus, who would view life and legend even more tragically, and would lay bare the ancient bogeys without long monologues, with a pitiless hand.

The driver couldn't be bothered to climb up to the palace, and took shelter in a patch of shade. He took out his cigarettes and offered one to the old watchman.

"C'mon," he said, "don't take it personally. . . ."

Alone I took the regal uphill path, which Clytemnestra had spread with precious red carpets on which her newly arrived husband might tread. "Step, step," she told him seductively, "don't fear the gods! *For happy victors too must yield. . . .*"

Along with the great shade I ascended, striding over the heat-warped paving stones of the palace; my glance swept over the surrounding mountains, the plain, far away to the gulf of the Argolid. I tried to visualize what Agamemnon saw as he went up toward his palace, and what his wife saw as, biting her lips, she scanned the distant sea for the hated ships of his return. They would have seen the same mountains, the same sun-baked plain, the same waves. But how they would have viewed them alone has significance. With what primordial fury.

Franz Mark, the German painter, was right when in trying to render a landscape viewed by a wild beast, he drew it as the beast would visualize it. And not as seen by the human eye. Thus he imagined it an amazing vision, flooded with color, dense, inexplicable, with no division between jungle and beast. You must climb up here to the palace of Agamemnon in the grip of a wild passion—hate, love, war, terror—in order to see the Argolid, the mountains and the sea as the Atreids would have seen them.

And in this way the tragedies of Aeschylus must be envisioned and staged. With just such an eye of the beast; the rest, classical balance, rhythmic choruses, gestures stylized from ancient earthen vessels, are all philology and soliloquizing sacrifices to Absent Aphrodite.

"What brigands, eh?" said the driver with admiration when I returned. "What grit! What brigands, eh? what bandits! Why today we're nothing but small-time crooks beside 'em."

■ PROBLEMS OF MODERN
GREEK CIVILIZATION

■ THE CIRCLE is closed, the gaze has made its round and enjoyed a bit of Greece. Mountains, fertile valleys, cities, villages, men, conversations, all crowd impatiently back into the mind, begging to be ordered in a total, to be organized, to find some meaning. As though travel were not disinterested delight for the eye, nor peregrination of the body, but rather a spiritual and intellectual leap, a search.

The calm gaze that is contented with the spectacle, with the mercurial, multicolored sensual surface, is no longer that of our time. Today we want to rip the veil, even if it be beautiful, to see the reality hidden behind, and to demand an explanation. Today's world seems unjust, beneath the aspirations of an honorable man; we wish to bring reality into close and faithful correspondence with our heart, to create new equilibrium. Only then, for a time at least, will the newly crystallized surface not conceal great contradictions; the so-called balanced, Classical era will come. Then the gaze will be able, as it travels, to look calmly upon the world. But until then, let us travel on searching, tearing the veil, suffering.

Travel renews the senses; things a thousand times repeated startle you as if seen for the first time. In the
cities and villages of the Peloponnesos, it seemed that
I saw for the first time the faces, the gestures, the figures
of my race. My memory filled with tiny, darting eyes,
with yellowed malarial visages, with movements charged
with animation, speed and avidity. But abruptly in the
taverns, at festivals, on holidays, once the superlogical,
self-obsessed petty merchants and evzones have had
a bit to drink, they burst into melancholy Oriental
amanés, into unexpected bitterness, revealing a soul
radically different from their sober, everyday soul.
Great riches, distant nostalgia, craving . . .

Digenes,[1] of Greek father and Oriental mother, is,
you feel, the symbolic hero of the race. Anxieties take
shape within you, difficult problems and daring hopes.
Just as the peoples of ancient Greece were a mixture of
the most varied races, young and old, European and
Oriental, so our own contemporary people, with its
great and unrelenting strength, has absorbed Slavs, Al-
banians, Franks, Arabs and Turks. A new blend. We
cannot claim to be an aged and venerable race. We are
young, our blood is still bubbling, unfermented must.

But we behave like old men, because one idea, persistent yet warranted, turns our eyes back, stimulates us
with great recollections, and causes us to concern ourselves and to live with things past, as if we were an aged
race. This persistent idea forms the foundation of our
national unity, whirling in its track and absorbing foreign blood.

I watch the merchants, the peasants, the house-holders, and their wives, their manners, their actions and reactions, and struggle to distinguish the two great currents which constitute the double-born soul of the modern Greek. And to inquire with fascination whether they have anywhere succeeded in reaching a synthesis. Thus, gazing over the Argolid, I head for Corinth, reviewing in my mind the principal attributes of the ancient forebear: love of life, calm confrontation of death, development of the body, harmony of flesh and mind, love of freedom, joyful attachment to the earth, with no longing for another, better world. And then opposite them I enumerate the attributes of that other ancestor, the Byzantine and Oriental: theocracy, feudalism, loathing of life, futility, pessimism, mysticism; he scorns this earth and wants to leave it, longing for a better, more enduring world.

What has the double-descended modern Greek taken from his father, what from his mother? We search for our new soul in demotic poetry, in dances, embroidery and music, in the architecture of the Greek house, in our habits, celebrations, sayings, superstitions and language; and we see the two currents, the native Greek and the Oriental, sometimes flowing side by side, never joining, sometimes meeting and struggling furiously, and even, rarely, joined in organic union. The modern Greek loves life and fears death, loves his homeland and is simultaneously a pathological individualist; he fawns upon his superiors like a Byzantine, and torments his inferiors like an Aga, yet he will die for his *filotimo*—his personal honor. He is clever and shallow, with no metaphysical anxieties, and yet, when he begins to sing, a universal grieving leaps up from his Oriental bowels and breaks the crust of Greek logic; all at once the East, all darkness and mystery, rises up from deep within him.

Walk through Greece, and wherever you stop, uneasy faces gather round you. As if they still remember the bloodshed, the savage Janissaries who toured the villages collecting the blood tribute, or the *kotzampashas*, the landed tyrants, who gathered the head tax. A foreigner is always viewed as a dangerous, suspicious presence; they must learn quickly who he is, what he intends to do, and take their measures. Even centuries later the blood remembers, the uneasiness has not disappeared. Time must elapse, sometimes a few seconds, sometimes days, for the primeval fear to be overcome, for the peasant's heart to open.

It is not only this ancient fear; it is the curiosity, the avidity of the Greek to learn, for nothing to evade him, to accumulate, to profit. This curiosity is a mild form of plunder and piracy, just as the kiss is a gentle sort of cannibalism. When the Greek reached his pinnacle, when he put to use, that is, all his shortcomings and aptitudes, the curiosity, gossip and agitation became Socratic dialogue and metaphysical quest: whence, where and why.

The journey was over, and as I awaited the train in the station at Argos, beneath the tall poplars, a young man in tourist garb set his knapsack down on the bench where I was seated and began a conversation. He wrote surrealistic poetry, and toured Europe, but now he'd been ensnared and had taken up his pack, his shorts and his staff to get a close look at Greece. Lofty, straying disposition, generosity and inability, spiritual purity and intellectual dislocation. He desired, but didn't even know what he could do. From word to word we approached the great problem which has started consciously to concern us, to nibble at us: How can we create, where can we build a modern Greek civilization of our own? He had read Dragoumis and Giannopoulos, he had studied Danielidis' profound book, he had discussed it among his friends, and reflected by himself; but his mind found no peace. Adoration of the ancients, blind acceptance of Europe, the East—he felt all these things within him, but they could find no harmony among themselves, and gave no cohesiveness to his life.

"And what do you have to say?"

I have often yielded to this question full-on; but the answer would spring up so impulsive, complex and impatient that I would be overcome. Today, though, the train was late in coming, the shade beneath the poplars was gentle and caressing, and the questioning of the youth was so genuine and disturbed, that for his sake I tried to give the answer some order, and to express my thoughts as clearly as I could.

"First of all," I answered him, "we must assume a correct and dignified position regarding the ancients. They are no longer our 'ancestors' alone; but those of the entire white race. No longer should we make ourselves ridiculous by glorying in the ancients as if they were our personal property, nor must we grovel before them like serfs. The ancestors have long since escaped the possession of any particular land and race; centuries ago they leaped from Greece to the West, mingled with new peoples, created a new civilization; they love and are loved by all who revere and understand them. Only for those are they true, deep ancestors. Indeed, I could also point out that no one understands their ancestors less well than the descendants. But this would take us far afield and we haven't the time.

"Western civilization, on the other hand, is an amazing attainment of modern man. It is our own contemporary; whether we like it or not we are caught up in its wheels, we've identified its destiny with our own. We eat, dress, house ourselves, act and think under its fearsome influence. There is no escape. No nation can escape any longer. Whichever attempts to flee is lost; all the other nations will swallow it. We are living the industrial civilization of our age, and it has no relation to either the Classical age of beauty, or to the metaphysical migration of the East.

"The problem of civilization is not as difficult and complicated for a nation of the West as it is for us. Naturally adapted to their native Western culture, they struggle solely to advance it, to endow it as much as possible with their own national nuance. But we are trapped between East and West. Greece's position, so they say, is a privileged one, but concurrently it is one of the world's most dangerous geographic and spiritual points. Within us exist profound powers opposed to the rhythm of the West. In order to create, we must reconcile terrible demons within us. What, then, is our duty?

"I can only define it in this rough way: The Orient, with its great, myriad cravings and its direct contact with the mystical substance of the world, will always form the warm, dark, rich subconscious of the Greek. The mission of the Greek mind has always been to illumine it, to organize it, to make it conscious. When it achieved this, it created what we call the Greek miracle. The Orient is the formless; the Greek mind has always been the force which loved and aspired toward one thing above all: form. To give form to the formless, to make reason of the Oriental cry; this is our duty. We can deny neither East nor West; both of these conflicting powers are deep within us, and cannot be extricated. We are obliged either to attain the distillation of East and West—in other words, to succeed in a very difficult synthesis—or to struggle on like slaves."

"A difficult task," said the youth.

"It happened once," I replied, and we stood up.

The train was coming. I bid the young man goodbye, laughing.

"Let all we've said be salt and water," I said. "Forget it. Don't be glum, don't dig about too deeply, abandon the theories. Otherwise you'll risk studying the problem without experiencing it. And only he who lives such problems can solve them. Don't suffer that which they tell to mock the learned, precise Germans: If they see two doors, on the one written 'Paradise' and on the other 'Lecture About Paradise,' they'll all rush for the second door.

"Experience within yourself all the powers that Greece has given you, labor day and night, manage to create a verse ripe with substance, with perfect form. Only thus will you solve the problem within your chosen field, and within that field create modern Greek civilization. Admire Dragoumis as I do. Let us bring a sentence of his to mind and repeat it now as we part: 'I often like to sense that I myself am one of the many passing archons of Hellenism, and that through me Hellenism must pass in order to carry on.' "

APPENDIXES

■ CHAPTER NOTES

SETTING OUT

1. Ion Dragoumis (1878-1920) exercised a strong influence on Kazantzakis' early years—preoccupation with the language question (demotic vs. puristic) and other national problems which found their first powerful expression in Dragoumis' life and work. He was victim of a political assassination.

2. The motto "Everything in excess" (*en agan*) was carved over the door of Kazantzakis' home in the island of Aigina.

THE GULF OF CORINTH

1. The *katostariko* was, and still is, the standard measure of wine in provincial Greece: a copper or enamel pot containing 100 drams.

THE FORTRESSES OF THE MOREA

1. Andreas Karkavitsas (1866-1922), born in Lekhaina, is one of Greece's foremost prose writers. His stories deal chiefly with provincial life—and by virtue of the author's strength, escape the limitations of folklore. Although Karkavitsas is almost unknown outside of Greece, his work holds a place nearly equal to that of Alexander Papadiamandis in modern Greek prose tradition. He wrote exclusively in demotic Greek.

2. Called Chlomoutsi or Chlemoutsi in Greek, the fortress was also known as Castel Tornese during the Middle Ages.

3. *Kafetzoudes* are old women who specialize in divining the future in the grounds left at the bottom of a coffee cup. They are also said to possess certain occult powers. The practice and its practitioners still flourish in rural Greece.

INSPIRATION OF THE LANDSCAPE

1. Perikles Giannopoulos (1872-1910), prolific hypernationalist writer and critic, was the favorite of Athenian romantics at the turn of the century. Although the Greek world of letters was shocked by his spectacular suicide, his works have since fallen into obscurity.

2. The Greek chivalrous verse romances owe their inspiration in large measure to the influence of the West. Some of them, indeed, are little more than adaptations of Frankish models.

MEDIEVAL GLARENZA

1. These lines, and those others which deal with the Frankish conquest of the Peloponnesos, are from the *Chronicle of the Morea*. Written in unrhymed "political" meter, apparently by a *gasmoulos* for the edification of the Greek-speaking Franks, it relates Villehardouin's exploits in the subjugation of the Morea.

2. Panait Istrati figured prominently in Kazantzakis' travels to Russia. The Rumanian-born writer of Greek descent was widely acclaimed throughout Europe in the 1920s. Kazantzakis describes their friendship in more detail in *Report to Greco*.

KARYTAINA, THE GREEK TOLEDO

1. Uneducated Greeks still refer to all Europeans as "Franks."

2. *Vrákes* are the baggy pantaloon-kilts which characterize the Cretan national costume.

THE OLD MAN OF THE MOREA

1. Kostis Palamas (1859-1941) is perhaps the greatest of modern Greek poets. His work embraces an astonishing span of subject matter. Kostas Karyotakis (1896-1928), like Giannopoulos in 1910, ended his life by suicide. His work, inferior to that of his master, Palamas, became the expression of a youthful generation of pessimism and despair. Konstantine Kavafis (1868-1933) is already widely known in the English-speaking world as one of the foremost poets of the early twentieth century.

2. Along with Palamas, Angelos Sikelianos (1884-1951) is one of the colossi of modern Greek literature. The verses quoted here form the introduction to the poem *From the Prologue of Plethon,*

in his collection, *Antidoro*. (1941) Sikelianos, who was a close friend of Kazantzakis, presented the verses to Helen Kazantzakis on her name day, and they later adorned the wall of the house in Aigina.

MISTRA

1. Mezythra, the original name for Mistra in the *Chronicle of the Morea*, resembles the Greek *myzythra*, a kind of cheese. Perhaps because the mountain on which the city is situated resembles a cheese.

MORTALS AND IMMORTALS

1. Fotis Kondoglou (1895-   ) has exercised a strong influence over modern Greek art. Kazantzakis admired, too, his literary production for its rich demotic language and rhythm—something of the atmosphere of the storytellers of Asia Minor.

2. Dimitris Papaflessas, an Orthodox priest, was one of the heroes of Greece's War of Independence.

THIRTY-THREE YEARS IN EARTH

1. From the poem *Taki-Ploumas* by Miltiadis Malakasis (1864-1943).

PROBLEMS OF MODERN GREEK CIVILIZATION

1. Digenes Akritas ("double-born," border guard of the Byzantine Empire), the warrior-hero of the Greek epic cycles and folk songs. Kazantzakis for a time had contemplated writing an *Akrita* of his own, rather as a sequel to his *Odyssey*; his plans were never fulfilled.

■ TRANSLATOR'S NOTE

■ In the prologue to the Greek edition of *Zorba the Greek*, Nikos Kazantzakis wrote: "Throughout my life, my greatest benefactors have been my dreams and my travels; very few men, living or dead, have helped me in my struggle . . ." He goes on to single out Homer, Bergson, Nietzsche and Zorba as those mortals whose influence has been most vital to his life and work. Some years later, shortly before his ill-fated last journey to the Orient, in an interview for the French Radio (recently published by Mme. Helen Kazantzakis in her epilogue to *Japan-China*), Kazantzakis was to unhesitatingly repeat precisely this thought.

Kazantzakis' great cohorts, the "bodyguards of the Odyssey" as he called them, along with a host of secondary, though by no means inferior figures, Christ, Lenin, Dante, Buddha, Greco, Psycharis and others, whom he enshrined in a series of *terza rima* cantos, helped enrich him with the formal means, the discipline, the example —he also called them his "models and guides"—for the technical consummation of his creation. But from his dreams and travels he drew the raw material of his work—the interplay and echo of ancestral cries in his own double-born soul; the meeting and mingling of European, African and Asian in his Cretan blood; the temperament at once withdrawing and passionate; the ability to gaze serenely for day after day at the seemingly endless wastes of Siberian steppe, to confront the exotic Orient, the blood-spattered body of Spain, the malaria-wracked face of the Peloponnesos.

Dream images abound in Kazantzakis' works—dreams provided him with a fruitful point of contact with subconscious currents which he might never have touched in his waking hours. Such images figure prominently in the superstructure of his *Odyssey*, as well as in innumerable more detailed incidents woven into its general fabric. And the entire closing section of *The Last Temptation of Christ* occurs in that dream state of suspended time which is one of Kazantzakis' favorite devices. In his dreams, logical fragments, components of thought as yet unorganized, would be caught up in the vortex of his subconscious and be given form at last, would ascend to knowledge's highest peak: to become vision.

Through dreams he maintained close contact with an entire world of childhood memory: the highly-charged atmosphere of Cretan freedom struggles; the forms of his parents, grandparents, ancestors; the soil and air of Crete itself. In a letter to his Swedish translator he wrote: "Just last night I dreamed that Crete sailed up and anchored like a ship outside of Antibes; I stretched out my leg, went aboard, and saw it all, from one end to the other; my joy was great."

Travel was, on the conscious level, what dreams were in his hours of sleep. Travel for Kazantzakis was far more than a mere changing of location, or a relief for heart and eye, a diversion. Travel is an agonizing quest, charged with hope and fear—all else in our age would be self-deceit and cowardice. He was to find in his travels the image that best expressed his soul, and hence his conception of the soul of contemporary man: Odyssey.

His own wanderings, in themselves a bewildering though not incoherent Odyssey, served a twofold purpose. First, as an occasion to make contact with the mercurial kaleidoscopic surface of the world, to plunge himself into the sensuousness of the moment, to sense in his soul the interplay of action and inaction, and then to grasp beneath the ephemeral surface, behind the brightly colored veil, the timeless manifestations of landscape, of man, of history petrified in marble. This contact was simultaneously the profoundest joy and greatest ordeal of his travels: ". . . let us travel on searching, tearing the veil, suffering."

Even though extremely shy, Kazantzakis was nevertheless able to refine his vision to the intensity of actual touch. His sense of penetration surpassed the limited perception of insatiable fingertips alone. He came to realize that the "eternity" which he sought in his vision was not a concept of quantity, either spatial or temporal, but rather of quality.

Second, travel was his greatest source, a rich font of impression, color, odor, sound and detail, all of which was stored away, catalogued, reworked and then brought back to find a place in his creation. Each journey became a search for material for his *Odyssey*. The wealth of an entire voyage accumulates in his mind as he finally confronts the merciless purpose: the blank sheet of paper.

From these two opposing tendencies the extraordinary pulse of Kazantzakis' travel books draws its strength. The confrontation of a soul which craves for an instant of touch and for the warmth of real flesh with the ascctic-artist who has set out to gather the multicolored booty of the sensible world and force it into submission beneath the patterns of his vision.

This conflict finds expression in the language and structure of the works themselves. Though written in a thoroughly "demotic" Greek, with a generous sprinkling of uncommon words, the books still very much reveal the desk-bound scholar; here we find a linc or two from an obscure document, from an unknown poet, there a metaphor or proverb drawn from a Muslim philosopher or a Byzantine mystic.

Journey to the Morea first appeared in serialized form in the Athenian newspaper *Kathimerini* in November and December of 1937. All of Kazantzakis' travel volumes, in fact, were first published in this manner: as reports from a "special correspondent." The actual journey upon which the book is based was made in September of that same year.

Perhaps more than any other of Kazantzakis' travel

books, *Journey to the Morea* escapes the limitations of a single voyage. He visited the Peloponnesos, for varying lengths of time, on five distinct occasions, and from the wealth of memory and incident inherent in this total, he was able to invest the *Journey* with unusual depth.

His first voyage to the "cradle of Hellenism" was in March 1915, in company with the great Greek lyric poet Angelos Sikelianos, whom Kazantzakis had just recently met in the offices of the Educational Society (a liberal-demoticist organization whose membership included some of the major figures of Greek political life and letters of the time—Ion Dragoumis, Kostas Várnalis, Lorenzo Mavílis). The two poets became acquainted in 1914, at once recognized a bond of shared interest between themselves, and immediately set out together for Athos, the Holy Mountain. After a stay of some months, during which they visited most of the monasteries of the Monk's republic, they wandered systematically through Greece, seeking, in the words of Sikelianos, the "conscience of their earth and race."

Kazantzakis visited the Morea with Sikelianos again in 1915, this time accompanied as well by his first wife, Galateia. Then in 1917, with Sikelianos and George Zorbas in the ill-fated lignite venture which was to become the subplot of *Zorba the Greek*. Again in 1922 the two poets toured the Morea, visiting Epidaurus, Mycenae, and Argos. Ten years later he returned with his old friend, the French journalist Renaud de Jouvenel.

The most significant detail in this chronology of

Journey to the Morea is its proximity to his great epic, *Odyssey*, which was completed in mid-1938 and published that December. The two-year period of 1937 and 1938 was an extremely rich one: In addition to the travel notes and his *magnum opus*, work on which had by then covered the course of twelve years, he also published his verse tragedy *Mélissa*, inspired by his visit to ancient Corinth.

Each of Kazantzakis' works should be viewed as the repetition, elaboration or elucidation of a concept or image from the *Odyssey*. The novels, the *Greek Passion*, *Freedom or Death*, the *Last Temptation* all embody one of the many germs of the Odyssean conception; the travel books to a lesser extent, without the same concentration. Here it is essential to clarify the often overlooked fact that Kazantzakis was a writer (and a man) of one single, all encompassing vision: Within the *Odyssey* can be found the points of departure for all his later novels. Through the novels Kazantzakis sought a level from which he might successfully address himself to a much broader readership than his poetry would have ever permitted—in their sum they do not exceed or unexpectedly alter the vision of the great work of his "acme" (as the ancient Greeks would have said). The travel books are of a different category: They do not elaborate, they prefigure.

Journey to the Morea abounds with these prefigurings of the *Odyssey*. As an example the sequence in Chapter X (The Enchantment of Sparta): Two representatives of strife-torn pre-Classic Greece journey to far-off India,

seeking the Word that will help them bring order to
their chaotic civilization. The sage who greets them so
ironically on the bank of the Ganges is none other than
Prince Motherth, the Buddha figure of the *Odyssey*. In
the face of his exhortations to nirvanic nothingness, the
Greeks plant firm in earth their image of Helen; to the
sly taunts of the sage they reply:

> "If Helen was but empty shade, may she be
> blessed!
> It's for this empty shade we fought with widen-
> ing minds;
> when old at length we turned back to our longed-
> for land,
> our minds crammed with adventures and with
> manly deeds . . ."
>
> (XXIV, 966-69)

Kazantzakis plays upon the eternal antithesis of
Greek thought, anthropomorphic and Apollonian, with
the formless abyss of the Orient. In the *Odyssey* the
younger of the Greeks is about to be ensnared by
Motherth's radiant, obliterating smile when the death
call of the dying Odysseus rends the air and an eagle
swoops down to carry the sage away. In the poem, the
seductive arguments of the sage follow the last admis-
sion of the Greeks:

> "Awake at last, uproot your wants, abjure your
> nightmares,

smother your hearts and your thick brains so they
    won't shout,
perk up your ears, for mountains, trees and waters
    roar:
'Come, come and merge as one with earth, with
    mother roots,
merge into one with sacred winds and the good
    showers!' "

                                     (XXIV, 987-91)

But in the *Journey* the Greeks' retort refutes the enticing sage and with assurance they answer: " 'Helen,' ascetic, means to do battle for Helen."

The reader senses Kazantzakis in the grip of an Odyssean predilection. The ship's master of Greece, Odysseus himself, appears atop Ionian waves at dusk after the roaring festival at Glarenza. The Spartan chapters reverberate with Odyssean overtones. Kazantzakis, for an instant, shares the certainty of his archer-hero: That sweet though the moments with Helen be, they alone are not that which he seeks; he knows that a beautiful woman means much more than erotic adventure. And at the same time he grasps, in her deathless aroma, in her image spread submissive at the feet of the Taygetos, a presence as palpable as that of the unknown woman "thirty-three years in earth."

Within the frugal confines of the *Journey* the reader will discover as well the foreshadowing of other familiar characters, tropes and images. The figure of the blind old Cretan, Perdikokostandi, appears, with slight modification, again and again in Kazantzakis' mature prose: as Zorba's grandfather (where Kolokotronis' tobacco episode also finds a place); as the regal, sensuous old monarch in *Mélissa* who mourns his passing from a world that teems with nubile maidens; as the figure of old Sifakas in *Freedom or Death*, who expires amid the last gathering of his venerable comrades-in-arms. And in the slender *santouri* player at the festival we catch a glimpse of one of the attributes of the immortal Zorba. These few indications should help illustrate to what extent Kazantzakis' method and vision is rooted in the soil of his dreams and travels, in the soil of Greece, and more, of Crete.

In his *Report to Greco* Kazantzakis describes an incident related to him by an aged Cretan villager: Fearsome corsairs, whose lairs long ago infested the rocky, precipitous shores of the great island, seized a boat bound from the East laden with a cargo of exotic spices. . . . Soon after, all Crete, from one tip to the other, reeked with the heady fragrance of cinnamon and nutmeg. Kazantzakis listened with delight; from that time on he was never to be without a stick of cinnamon and two or three pieces of nutmeg—keeping them with him in his travels, and before him atop his desk as he wrote.

Journey to the Morea will perhaps serve to help clarify Kazantzakis' relation to his native land. While certain sections of it find a place, albeit highly revised, in *Report to Greco*, there they lack the same systematic context. Furthermore it should be stressed that the

Report makes no claim to chronological exactitude—events and images are given free play, virtually ideal form. In the *Journey*, partially due to the scrupulously observed external format, Kazantzakis' feelings and judgments about Greece are more objectively accessible; thus they can be readily, and no less truthfully, evaluated.

That which in the end will most certainly impress the reader of the *Journey* is its remarkable faculty for grasping the broad span of history—not coldly, with a scholarly, measured stride, but with a single fiery, engaged and penetrating glance, a glance rooted always in the uneasiness of the present. Kazantzakis is not afraid to declare that he cannot easily sense the ancient temples; far more than the now inert stones, a phrase from a living mouth, recalling the unbroken and eternal bond between man and the Greek earth, fills his heart. This he requires of modern Greece: correspondence of man and landscape, and further, realization of the path that Greece must follow, midway between the treacherous influences of East and West—synthesis or abject submission to a fate untrue to its nature.

Travel in the Peloponnesos reveals to him with frightening intensity the pitiful plight of his race. With the same eye that has feasted on the riches of the Orient and gazed at Russia's interminable snowy expanse, he now searches about him trying to discover Greece's true face, among the malaria-stricken peasants and the stagnant-souled householders of the provinces. From this dismal bog several great shades leap up, as if to console him: the swashbuckling Villehardouins of the Frankish conquest, who left the landscape of the Morea dotted with their still-forbidding fortresses, and with blond-headed, blue-eyed children; Gemistos Plethon, the renowned neoplatonist philosopher of Mistra; Kolokotronis, one of the fathers of modern Greece.

The reader will begin to understand why Kazantzakis was finally unable to make his home in Greece: A soul such as his could not be accommodated; his inner demands outstripped contemporary possibility. The brief and fruitless sojourn as minister without portfolio in the Sofoulis government of 1945 and 1946 proved with finality the impossibility of practical application of his idealist, liberal political thought; the petty intrigues of his enviers befouled the atmosphere of Greek letters. Only from a distance could Kazantzakis—realizing at last the unavoidable dictum—continue to devote himself to his creative work, upon which he knew his salvation depended.

Kazantzakis traveled through Greece seeking those souls, those landscapes, that would inspire him with courage and confidence in his homeland. Sensing profoundly the currents of his age (the reader of today will find Kazantzakis' *Odyssey* pertinent as never before), he wandered much of the turmoil-ridden world. In Greece he was not fated to see the wild conflict of contemporary man's soul, as he did in Spain; but rather to feel anguish, and isolation. He sought there fulfillment of the Greek ideal, and behind that, we sense as well, the paradox-rich lucidity of the Cretan

Glance. Only once or twice in his journey could he exclaim: "Suddenly a soul leaps up before you which has reached the peak of the Greek mission—to unite boldness with knowledge, passion with the game."

■ ACKNOWLEDGMENT

■ The translator wishes to express his gratitude to Mme. Helen Kazantzakis for her unfailing aid in the solution of certain technical problems and for her ready encouragement and advice. He also wishes to thank Mr. Aristotle Grammatikakis, Mr. N. Krasadakis, Mayor of Iraklion, Crete, and Mr. Lefteris Skoulas, indefatigable, narghile-smoking hotel-keeper of that city, for their kindness and interest, in so greatly facilitating work during his stay there. Finally, he owes a great debt of thanks to Mr. Kostas Grammatikakis and to Mr. Manolis Rousakis for their enthusiastic support, and to Mr. W. Patrick Milburn, to whom this translation is dedicated.

F. A. Reed

Iraklion, Crete
Montreal